Managing America's Small Communities

Managing America's Small Communities

People, Politics, and Performance

David H. Folz
and P. Edward French

ROWMAN & LITTLEFIELD PUBLISHERS, INC.
Lanham • Boulder • New York • Toronto • Oxford

ROWMAN & LITTLEFIELD PUBLISHERS, INC.

Published in the United States of America
by Rowman & Littlefield Publishers, Inc.
A wholly owned subsidiary of The Rowman & Littlefield Publishing Group, Inc.
4501 Forbes Boulevard, Suite 200, Lanham, Maryland 20706
www.rowmanlittlefield.com

PO Box 317
Oxford
OX2 9RU, UK

British Library Cataloguing in Publication Information Available

Library of Congress Cataloging-in-Publication Data

Folz, David H.
Managing America's small communities : people, politics, and performance /
David H. Folz and P. Edward French.
        p. cm.
Includes bibliographical references and index.
ISBN 0-7425-4338-2 (cloth : alk. paper)—ISBN 0-7425-4339-0 (pbk. : alk. paper)
1. Local government—United States.   2. Mayors—United States.   3. Municipal
government by city manager—United States.   4. Municipal services—United States.
5. Total quality management in government—United States.   I. French, P. Edward,
1964–   II. Title.   JS356.F65   2005
352.16—dc22

                                                                   2005006725
Printed in the United States of America

♾ ™ The paper used in this publication meets the minimum requirements of American
National Standard for Information Sciences—Permanence of Paper for Printed Library
Materials, ANSI/NISO Z39.48-1992.

For my wife, Brenda Folz, a precious gift from God whose love, patience, and support made it possible for me to devote the time to write this book

For my wife Amy, daughter Amanda, and parents Margaret H. French and the late Jack P. French

Contents

List of Illustrations

FIGURES

TABLES

Acknowledgments

This research would have been impossible without the cooperation of numerous mayors and city managers in small communities across the United States who took the time to respond to a lengthy survey instrument. A special debt of gratitude also is owed to several individuals who gave generously of their time. Dennis Gage, manager with the Natural Hazards and Risk Decision Services division of the Insurance Services Office, collected and shared the ISO's data on municipal fire protection and building code enforcement service classifications for all of the small communities in this study. Colleagues at the University of Tennessee Municipal Technical Advisory Service provided critical information for and feedback on various aspects of this research. Special thanks to Alan Major, Ron Darden, Ray Crouch, Rex Barton, and Bob Schwartz. The professional staff for the respective municipal benchmarking programs also provided valuable insights about their projects. Thanks to David Ammons and Bill Rivenbark with the University of North Carolina Institute of Government, Anna Berger with the University of South Carolina Institute for Public Service and Policy Research, and Shalen Hunter with the Northwest Municipal Conference. Ms. Kelly McGuire, my UT MPA graduate assistant, helped to collect community data from secondary sources.

Finally, a very special thanks to Brenda Folz, Norman Couns, and Betty Folz for their careful editorial scrutiny and advice that helped to improve the readability of the text.

1

Introduction

Small communities have a special, if somewhat paradoxical, place in American life and political culture. Depicted as the wellsprings of faith, patriotism, and individualism as well as community spirit, small towns have attained almost mythic status in Americans' quest for a better quality of life and a safer, friendlier place in which to live, work, and raise kids. Portrayed as backward hamlets where the only change one gets is from a dollar bill used to pay for a moon pie and RC cola, small towns are viewed with some suspicion, as places that harbor old prejudices and practices long discredited by others.[1] In between these two stereotypical extremes lies the reality of small town life and politics and a large segment of the American political landscape and public management world that scholars in public administration have not studied systematically.

From the windswept plains of west Texas to the rolling green hills of east Tennessee to the bustling corridors of the nation's suburbs, many small communities are indeed blessed with the people, assets, and attributes that help make them highly attractive places to live. Yet there is a lot more to the social and political fabric of small towns than quiet neighborhoods, quaint residents, Friday night football, and regular meetings by the local elite at their table in the downtown diner or café. Many small communities face challenges and changes every bit as serious and daunting as those that confront their larger counterparts but that typically receive more publicity. Small size does not necessarily mean that problems are small scale. Indeed, the leaders and managers of small communities may have one of the toughest and most demanding jobs in public service.

With very limited budgets and staff, small town officials are expected to provide basic services that protect and advance residents' health, safety, and welfare and also to do "something" to mitigate the panoply of negative forces that may threaten community sustainability. Typical action agenda items include a crumbling infrastructure, an influx of residents that overwhelms the capacity of services and facilities, an exodus of citizens in search of jobs, the ravages inflicted by the insidious spread of methamphetamine labs, or the acute needs that arise in the wake of a tragedy of natural or human origin. Other concerns include strains on the local property tax, an influx of immigrants, or a popular reluctance to pay more for services.

The challenges involved in effectively managing the contemporary small community are impressive, but so too are the opportunities that may arise for individual public servants to make a positive difference in residents' lives and community sustainability. While most small towns lack the fiscal resources and political clout in state politics enjoyed by larger cities, their officials often are in a better strategic position to understand citizens' needs, exercise community leadership, and devise creative solutions for service pressures and problems.[2]

The downside to greater familiarity is that small town local officials are under a community magnifying glass, or as one mayor who will remain unnamed put it, "just about everybody in town knows when you screw-up." Still, how well small city chief executives execute the burdens of leadership and fulfill expectations for local services depends in large part on their vision, skills, abilities, and education as well as the structure and features of the local governmental process in which they operate.[3] Undoubtedly, bold executive leadership and efficient and effective service delivery in small communities are complicated by reliance on an obsolete tax base, pressures for more services but a popular unwillingness to pay for them, and unfunded federal and state mandates.[4]

Those who heed a calling to public service in a small community are perhaps a breed apart. They must be prepared to tackle some very tough problems with very limited resources while operating in a fishbowl of scrutiny by the local press and public.[5] The conditions, features, constraints, and opportunities that characterize the leadership and management of small city governments and the results achieved by the dedicated cadre of public servants who work in this arena certainly merit a lot more attention from scholars than they have received. The deficit of scholarly analyses of issues related to the governance and management of small cities is regrettable but understandable, especially considering the limited data collected by governmental and professional organizations on cities with less than 25,000 people.

This book charts several key aspects of the largely unexamined world of small city governments and the services they provide. Among the questions and issues examined are the demographic trends, structural features, and executives of small communities. Are small cities growing, are they declining, or have they remained untouched by the forces of change that affect the rest of the nation? To what extent have the winds of structural change and reform that have swept through larger cities touched small communities? What are the characteristics and behavior of small city chief executives? What sort of people are attracted to run for mayor and to serve as city managers? On what activities do these executives spend their time? How involved are they in the different dimensions of the local governmental process, and what are the implications of their respective levels of involvement? How do chief executives make decisions about local services and programs, and are there any differences between mayors and city managers with respect to how responsive they are to community interest groups?

This book also examines several aspects of the services provided in small communities. Among the issues examined are the frequency with which small communities provide various services, what quality of services they provide, how and why service quality should be measured, and how small city officials can diagnose problems with service quality and performance. We also identify the factors that help to explain some of the differences in the level of service quality in four services commonly provided by small cities. Finally, this text explains the value of measuring and comparing service performance by small communities and summarizes the experiences of contemporary municipal performance benchmarking projects in order to highlight what small city officials can learn from these collective municipal experiences about measuring service performance and sharing ideas to help improve services.

The thematic glue that binds the examination of these questions and issues is the value added to small communities that evidence professionalism in city administration. Whenever the evidence warrants, we highlight the benefits that accrue to those communities that have the services of a city manager or a full-time chief administrative officer (CAO). This thematic focus does not diminish the importance of the contributions made by talented mayors who may share the same orientation as professionals. Executives who have a professional orientation to city administration typically base their policy and service strategies on needs rather than demands, emphasize the long-term interests of the community as a whole, promote fairness and equality, and advance broad and inclusive participation by citizens.[6]

It became apparent in the early stages of this research that the type of municipal executive helped to distinguish particular outcomes that were perceived to add value to the governance and management of small communities.[7] As the reader will discover in the subsequent chapters, the added value of having a professional manager or CAO is most apparent with respect to their level of involvement in the various dimensions of the governmental process, their broader pattern of consultation in making decisions, their level of responsiveness to community interests, and the level of input service quality provided by small communities. In addition, while relatively few small communities currently use performance measures, those with city managers and CAOs are more inclined to see the value of performance measurement and management systems.[8] Accordingly, these executives are likely to be interested in the performance measures that have survived the crucible of several years of review and refinement by teams of service managers involved in municipal benchmarking programs.

WHY STUDY SMALL COMMUNITIES?

While the residents of small cities have no illusions about where they live, a review of the urban politics and public administration literature might suggest that they are part of a "lost world" of American politics. Previous research on local government executive leadership and municipal services has focused almost exclusively on larger cities and on the behaviors of either city managers or mayors in these jurisdictions.[9] Few studies have examined both mayors and city managers, and none has explicitly focused on the governance and management of small communities.[10]

The paucity of academic research on the management and governance of small communities borders on the scandalous, especially considering that these cities comprise the vast majority of all incorporated U.S. municipalities. In 2003, for example, there were 7,036 cities with populations larger than 2,500 people. Of this number, 5,631 or 80 percent had populations between 2,500 and 25,000, the population range of communities that are the focus of this research.[11] Moreover, these small communities were home to about one-third of the nation's urban population and employed about two-thirds (64.44 percent) of the ICMA's 2,796 professional city managers.[12] Despite the large proportions they comprise of all municipalities and of employed city managers, little is known about the structure of political power and authority in these small communities, the behavior of their executive leaders, and the types and quality of services they provide.

This knowledge deficit is especially troubling for graduate MPA faculty, who may have several students who aspire to positions in municipal administration. For those who find job opportunities with small cities and suburbs, are they leaving campus with the idea that the challenges of managing a small community are not much different than those that confront executives in large cities? Do they think that small town issues and problems are just a microcosm of those on the agendas of their metropolitan counterparts, which dominate the public administration literature?

Small communities also are where many city administrators, for a variety of reasons, begin and choose to remain for most or all of their careers. How much of what scholars advocate about the need for systematic program planning, performance measurement, performance budgeting, and service evaluation, for example, is germane to the environment of pervasive austerity in which these administrators typically function?

Systematic study of the issues related to the governance and management of small communities is long overdue. This work is a modest effort to help broaden and advance our understanding of some of the key dimensions of executive behavior, service delivery, and service evaluation in small cities. Much work remains to be done. Suggestions for future research are described in the final chapter.

PURPOSE OF THE BOOK

This book aims to begin the process of filling the large gap in our knowledge about the governance and management of small communities. The intended audience includes students, practitioners, and scholars in public administration and urban politics. Students interested in a career in city management and who may consider launching their public service careers with a smaller local government will begin their service with a clearer understanding of the issues important to small communities, the emerging trends in the structural features of small city government, the decision-making processes of different types of chief executives, how to measure the quality of services provided, and how to diagnose potential problems with service quality and performance.

Seasoned practitioners in small communities understand that, in the end, what really matters in the political environment in which they operate is performance, the ability to achieve desired results.[13] Accordingly, managers should find some merit in the clarification of the concept of service quality and the illustrations of the range of service quality dimensions that may shape citizen and client perceptions of service quality. Practitioners who want to measure service performance in their communities should find value in the summaries of the performance measurement and comparison experiences of cities that have participated in the major U.S. benchmarking programs.

Scholars in public administration are challenged to give more attention to the measurement of both the input and output dimensions of municipal service quality as part of municipal service analyses. Devising more refined operationalizations of input quality for various services will help to facilitate more comparable, useful, and fairer municipal service performance comparisons. Scholars also are challenged to advance and refine the conceptual model of service quality presented and to test the utility of gap analyses in diagnosing potential problems with local service performance. Finally, there are several lessons and implications discerned from the experiences of contemporary benchmarking efforts that scholars should consider in the design of future municipal benchmarking projects.

DATA AND METHODS

The source for information about small city executives, their decision-making processes, and their behavior is a national mail survey that was conducted by P. Edward French, involving a random, stratified sample of 1,000 chief executives in U.S. cities with populations between 2,500 and 24,500, in fall 2000.[14] The sample was stratified proportionately by region and form of government. The four geographic regions were Northeast, South, Midwest, and West. For the purposes of this research, only cities with either a mayor-council or council-manager form of government structure were included in the target population. The source used to identify cities, their region, and their form of government was the International City/County Management Association's (ICMA) 1999 *Municipal Yearbook*.[15]

Two follow-up mailings were administered after the initial fall 2000 mailing, and by early 2001 valid responses had been received from a total of 508 chief executives, confirmed as being either mayors in mayor-council cities or city managers in council-manager cities. The response rate to the survey was 51 percent. The mail survey required respondents to identify the specific position that they held in the city government. Any survey responses completed by someone other than the mayor or city manager were excluded from the analysis. The 508 responses included in this study were verified as being completed by a mayor or city manager.

Table 1.1 shows the distribution of survey responses by region and form of government compared to the distributions for all of the cities in the target population. There is a very close correspondence between the sample returns and the proportions of the target population that have a mayor-council and council-manager form of government. Likewise, the regional distribution of cities in the returned surveys and in the target population is comparable. The only cell in the table that is overrepresented in the sample is the proportion of mayors from the West.

Overall, the returns from the mail survey reflect the distributions of all small U.S. cities by form of government and region. Generalizations about the target population of small U.S. cities based on our sample are possible with a 4.5 percent error margin at the 95 percent level of confidence.

Table 1.1. Small City Target Population and Survey Returns by Region and Form of Government, 2000

| | Mayor-Council Cities | | | | Council-Manager Cities | | | |
| | Target Population | | Survey Returns | | Target Population | | Survey Returns | |
Region	N	Percent	N	Percent	N	Percent	N	Percent
NE	900	32.5	67	25.0	518	21.3	51	21.3
S	748	27.0	73	27.2	830	34.2	80	33.3
MW	935	33.7	65	24.3	638	26.3	64	26.7
W	190	6.8	63	23.5	443	18.2	45	18.7
Totals	2,773	100.0	268	100.0	2,429	100.0	240	100.0
By form	2,773	53.3	268	52.8	2,429	46.7	240	47.2

The data for the various demographic, social, and economic features of small cities were derived from various U.S. government documents such as the U.S. Censuses in 1990 and 2000 and the County-City data book. The information on the attributes of city services was obtained from several sources. Fire suppression ratings for the cities in the study were obtained directly from the national headquarters of the Insurance Services Office. Police staffing data in 1999 were obtained from reports issued by the Federal Bureau of Investigation. Information on the attributes of recycling programs was collected by contacting each municipality by e-mail or telephone to ascertain the features of any recycling program operated by the community in 1999.

PLAN FOR THE BOOK

Chapter 2 summarizes the key features of small communities and the characteristics of their chief executives. Understanding the social, economic, and political aspects of small towns helps to place in perspective the management challenges that confront chief executives.

Chapter 3 examines several questions of long-standing interest to public administration scholars in particular. These concern whether there are any substantively important differences between the different types of chief executives and the types of governmental structures in which they operate with respect to how executives allocate their time, how involved they are in the various dimensions of the governing process, how they make decisions, and how responsive they are to the concerns of community interests in making decisions about local services.

Chapter 4 focuses on the quality of services provided by small communities, how to measure the concept of service quality, and how managers can use this information. The two dimensions of service quality, input and output, are discussed, and a conceptual model illustrates the relationship between these two dimensions and the factors and gaps that may affect how citizens and clients perceive service quality. A case is presented for the importance of measuring input service quality. In addition, indicators are suggested for measuring the important dimensions of output service quality. Proximate measures of input service quality are used to identify three levels of input service quality for police, fire, building inspections, and recycling services. The factors that help to explain why communities have different levels of input service quality are identified.

Chapter 5 describes the importance of measuring service performance in small cities and the information that different types of measures can provide. It summarizes the operation and experiences of contemporary municipal benchmarking projects, extracts implications for future benchmarking projects, and describes those elements that can help to advance the practice of performance measurement and management among small cities. Interviews with staff for these benchmarking projects helped to identify the performance measures that participating cities found to be particularly meaningful in quantifying service workload, efficiency, and effectiveness.

Chapter 6 summarizes the study's findings and conclusions and suggests directions for future research on the governance and management of small communities. Appendix A indicates the specific types of measures used by cities that participate in four major municipal benchmarking projects. Appendix B contains the types and definitions of financial data collected from cities that participate in the Tennessee Municipal Benchmarking Project.

NOTES

1. The paradoxical portrayal of small communities in the media has been documented by the University of Minnesota Center for Small Towns. See, for example: Benjamin Winchester, *Media Messages of Rural: Lessons from Minnesota* (Morris: University of Minnesota Center for Small Towns, 2004).

2. James R. Bowers and Wilbur C. Rich, eds., *Governing Middle-Sized Cities: Studies in Mayoral Leadership* (Boulder, Colo.: Rienner, 2000).

3. James H. Svara, *Official Leadership in the City: Patterns of Conflict and Cooperation* (Oxford: Oxford University Press, 1990).

4. David R. Morgan and Robert E. England, *Managing Urban America* (New York: Chatham House, 1999).

5. Gordon Chase and Elizabeth C. Reveal, *How to Manage in the Public Sector* (Boston: McGraw-Hill, 1983).

6. See James H. Svara, "Do We Still Need Model Charters? The Meaning and Relevance of Reforms in the 21st Century," *National Civic Review* 90, no.1 (2001): 19–33; William H. Hansell, "Professionalism in Local Government Administration," in *The Future of Local Government Administration: The Hansell Symposium*, ed. H. George Frederickson and John Nalbandian, 181–92 (Washington, D.C.: ICMA Press, 2002).

7. See P. Edward French and David H. Folz, "Executive Behavior and Decision Making in Small U.S. Cities," *American Review of Public Administration* 34, no.1 (2004): 52–66.

8. A national survey of chief administrative officers conducted by Yeonsoo Chung and David H. Folz at the University of Tennessee, Knoxville, during the summer and fall of 2004 indicated that chief executives in "administrative" and "adaptive" cities were much more likely than mayors in "political" cities to have adopted and actually used performance measures for at least some municipal services. An executive summary of these survey results for cities of moderate size is available upon request from dfolz@utk.edu.

9. The scholarly focus on executive management of political conflict and cooperation and on local services is entirely appropriate since these are the two major functions of a city in American politics. Examples of studies that have examined executive behavior in larger cities include Charldean Newell and David N. Ammons, "Role Emphases of City Managers and Other Municipal Executives," in *Ideal and Practice In Council-Manager Government*, ed. H. George Fredrickson, 97–107 (Washington, D.C.: ICMA Press, 1995); Richard C. Kearney and Carmine Scavo, "Reinventing Government in Reformed Municipalities: Manager, Mayor and Council Actions," *Urban Affairs Review* 37, no. 1 (2001): 43–66; James H. Svara, "Dichotomy and Duality: Reconceptualizing the Relationship Between Policy and Administration in Council-Manager Cities," *Public Administration Review* 45, no. 1 (1985): 221–32; James H. Svara, *Official Leadership in the City*; James H. Svara, "The Shifting Boundary Between Elected Officials and City Managers in Large Council-Manager Cities," *Public Administration Review* 59, no. 1 (1999): 44–53; Deil S. Wright, "The City Manager as a Development Administrator," in *Comparative Urban Research*, ed. Robert T. Daland, 203–48 (Beverly Hills, Calif.: Sage, 1969); Robert L. Lineberry and Edmund P. Fowler, "Reformism and Public Policies in American Cities," *American Political Science Review* 61, no. 3 (1967): 701–16; Albert K. Karnig, "Private-Regarding Policy, Civil Rights Groups, and the Mediating Impact of Municipal Reforms," *American Journal of Political Science* 19, no. 1 (1975): 91–106; Susan B. Hansen, "Participation, Political Structure, and Concurrence," *American Political Science Review* 69, no. 4 (1975): 1181–99; Thomas R. Dye and John A. Garcia, "Structure, Function, and Policy in American Cities," *Urban Affairs Quarterly* 14, no. 1 (1978): 103–23; Paul Schumaker and Russell W. Getter, "Structural Sources of Unequal Responsiveness to Group Demands in American Cities," *The Western Political Quarterly* 36, no. 1 (1983): 7–29; and Paul E. Mouritzen and James H. Svara, *Leadership at the Apex:*

Politicians and Administrators in Western Local Governments (Pittsburgh, Pa.: University of Pittsburgh Press, 2002).

10. The only text that focuses on small city and county services is James M. Banovetz, Drew A. Dolan, and John W. Swain, *Managing Small Cities and Counties: A Practical Guide* (Washington, D.C.: ICMA Press, 1994); see also David A. Booth, *Council-Manager Government in Small Cities* (Washington, D.C.: ICMA Press, 1968).

11. International City/County Management Association, *The Municipal Yearbook* (Washington, D.C.: ICMA Press, 2003)

12. Avon Pagon, staff member International City/County Management Association, e-mail message to author, October 19, 2004.

13. Chase and Reveal, *How to Manage in the Public Sector.*

14. The mail survey was implemented with the generous assistance of the John C. Stennis Institute of Government at Mississippi State University.

15. International City/County Management Association, *The Municipal Yearbook* (Washington, D.C.: ICMA Press, 1999).

2

Profile of Small Communities and Chief Executives

What are the main characteristics and features of the people, government, and leaders of America's small cities? How do these compare with the rest of the nation? To what extent have small towns embraced changes in government structure similar to those adopted by larger cities? This chapter summarizes the notable demographic, social, economic, and governmental features of small U.S. cities and the characteristics of their chief executives.

DEMOGRAPHIC TRENDS IN SMALL COMMUNITIES

Between 1990 and 2000, the nation's population increased about 13.15 percent, with the West and South realizing larger population gains than the Northeast and Midwest. These national and regional trends always tend to mask the demographic stories of individual communities. Cities within each region may confront diverse challenges linked to rapid growth, population loss, or stasis. Some communities faced development pressures and service demands that threatened to diminish the assets that made them attractive places to live and work in the first place. Other cities struggled to remain viable political and financial entities because of out-migration, downtown decay, employment base erosion, or environmental constraints. Still other cities remained virtually unchanged in population size but encountered new service challenges linked to the evolving needs of their populations. What about small cities? Are they generally growing, losing population, or staying pretty much the same size?

The stereotypical image of American small towns as sleepy hamlets in which the closest mall is more than an hour's drive away and where dating choices are limited mainly to the ex-boyfriend or ex-girlfriend of one's best friend is an enduring one. While small town shopping and dating choices may still be limited, population changes in small communities may auger wider choices in the future. During the 1990–2000 decade, most small communities experienced population growth that was larger in percentage terms than that realized by the nation as a whole. On average, the population of all small cities (those between 2,500 and 25,000 in 1990) increased by 16.3 percent by 2000. The mean population size rose to 10,075 from 8,585 during this period.

About 70 percent of small cities gained at least one hundred people during the 1990s, and the mean increase experienced by those cities that gained population was 2,181 people. Only 20 percent of small cities lost more than one hundred people during the 1990–2000 decade. The average decline for these cities was 584 people. About 10 percent of small cities experienced little change in population size (neither gaining nor losing more than one hundred people).

Following national trends, small communities in each geographic region generally gained population. Cities in the West and South experienced the largest gains (averaging 2,358 and 1,652, respectively) while those in the Midwest and Northeast averaged smaller population gains (876 and 202, respectively). Each region experienced substantial increases in their Hispanic population, with the largest gains occurring in the West, South, and Midwest. In 2000, Hispanics comprised 24.3 percent of the population in the West, 11.6 percent in the South, and 4.9 percent in the Midwest.

Popular images of the little town on the prairie or the tiny village in the hollow are increasingly inaccurate characterizations of the contemporary small community. The reality is that many small cities are less isolated and less independent than ever before. Many have become exurbs, indistinguishable from the tentacles of growth that have enveloped them. Remarkably, the 2000 census indicated that the majority (57.5 percent) of small cities were located *within* the boundaries of either a metropolitan or micropolitan statistical area. The expanding wave of U.S. urbanization has touched many small towns that were once more isolated, independent communities. In fact, between 1990 and 2000, the percent of the U.S. population that resided in rural areas, as defined by the U.S. Census Bureau, declined from 25 to 21 percent. The occurrence of independent small cities located *outside* of one of the Census Bureau's designated "core-based" statistical urban areas is rapidly fading from the American demographic landscape.

Tracking demographic changes is always made more interesting by changes that occur in the terminology used by the U.S. Census Bureau. For the 2000 census, the Census Bureau began to use a new definition of an "urban cluster" called a *micropolitan statistical area*. A micropolitan statistical area is "a core-based statistical area that has at least one urban cluster of at least 10,000, but less than 50,000 people."[1] A micropolitan area may encompass a central county and any adjacent counties "that have a high degree of social and economic integration with the central county as measured through commuting."[2] A *metropolitan statistical area* is a "core-based statistical area that has at least one urbanized area of at least 50,000 plus adjacent counties that have a high degree of social and economic integration with the central county as measured through commuting."[3]

As indicated in table 2.1, about 7.3 percent of all small cities were located in a micropolitan area and over half (50.2 percent) of all small cities were located in a metropolitan statistical area in 2000. Consequently, by 2000 the majority of small town residents were living in areas that the U.S. Census defined as more urban than rural in character.

As suburban, exurban, and edge city growth continues apace, many once independent small towns now find themselves becoming the locations of choice for businesses seeking less expensive land, lower taxes, or a lighter regulatory burden. Likewise, more Americans appear to prefer living in smaller communities that they perceive as providing a more affordable, safer, and pleasant quality of life.[4] Accordingly, America's once more numerous independent small cities are becoming part of a broader, more widely dispersed pattern of urbanization. For local officials, more residents usually means more pressure on services, facilities, and infrastructure. Unmanaged, these pressures can contribute to problems related to sprawl, congestion, pollution, and crime.

The social profile of small cities indicates a general pattern of homogeneity. Small towns have a smaller proportion of nonwhites, a lower median household income, and a lower median value for owner-occupied housing than the nation as a whole. While the proportion of people with high school diplomas (or equivalent) is about the same as that for the entire nation (about 80 percent), the proportion of small town residents with a college degree is significantly lower than the national average. Only about 15 percent of small town residents twenty-five or older have a bachelor's degree, compared to about 25 percent of all citizens.

In terms of education spending, small communities spend less than the national average on K–12 public education even though they have a somewhat smaller pupil-teacher ratio than the national average. The mean per pupil expenditure among small cities is about 9 percent less than the national average but that expenditure gap does not appear to translate into a large difference in educational achievement, at least according to one measure of that concept.[5]

Table 2.1. Features of Small U.S. Communities, 2000 National Survey

Characteristic	N	Percent
1990 population distribution		
Less than 5,000	164	36.9
5,000 to 9,999	136	30.6
10,000 to 14,999	77	17.3
15,000 to 19,999	44	9.9
20,000 to 25,000	24	5.4
Total	445	100.0
2000 population distribution		
less than 5,000	144	28.3
5,000 to 9,999	162	31.9
10,000 to 14,999	84	16.5
15,000 to 19,999	60	11.8
20,000 to 25,000	58	11.4
Total	508	100.0
1990 population mean	8,585	
2000 population mean	10,075	
Mean population change 1990–2000 (N=445)	+1,400	+16.3
Lost 100 or more people 1990–2000	91	20.4
Neither lost or gained more than 100 people 1990–2000	44	9.9
Gained more than 100 people 1990–2000	310	69.7
Classification as nonmetropolitan, 2000 (survey cities)	216	42.5
Classification as micropolitan, 2000 (survey cities)	37	7.3
Classification as metropolitan, 2000 (survey cities)	255	50.2
Mean 2000 population of mayor-council cities	8,717	52.8
Mean 2000 population of council-manager cities	11,592	47.2
Mean 2000 population in "political cities"	8,930	63
Mean 2000 population in "adaptive cities"	9,557	281
Mean 2000 population for "administrative cities"	11,402	164
Mean population change 1990–2000 in "political cities"	+604	62
Mean population change 1990–2000 in "adaptive cities"	+1,322	244
Mean population change 1990–2000 in "administrative cities"	+1,892	139

	Small Cities	U.S.
Percent nonwhite population	15.81	24.9
Median household income (1999)	41,525	41,994
Median year structure built	1966	
Median value for owner-occupied housing	112,249	119,600
Mean municipal land area (sq. miles)	8.43	n.a.
Population density	1999.85	
Percent high school graduates	79.4	80.4
Percent persons 25 & older with at least a bachelor's degree	14.7	24.4
Education Achievement index*	4.82	5.1
K–12 Expenditures per pupil	$5,488.50	$5,928
Pupil-teacher ratio in public schools	17.3	17.7

* Sperling's Index (1 through 10 where 10 is highest); n.a. = not available.

STRUCTURAL FEATURES OF SMALL TOWN GOVERNMENTS

Most public administration scholars believe that governmental structure and form matter for a variety of reasons.[6] How power and authority in local government are structured, for example, shapes the nature and process of decision making and represents an authoritative allocation of values.[7] The structure of local government also affects citizens' access to decision-making arenas, the ability of different interests to achieve their goals, and consequently what policies emerge from the governmental process. Government structure may reflect dominant community expectations and values about how the local government ought to function, what responsibilities it has, what services it should provide, and who should pay for these services. The perceived legitimacy of a government may depend in part on the extent to which a city's government conforms to these expectations.[8] As community expectations and values evolve or shift in emphasis, some cities may respond by changing their structure of governance.

Just as national and state constitutions represent the rules of the "governmental game," a municipal charter specifies the powers, organization, and form of local government. Municipal charters function much like a local constitution. The requirements for creating a city charter and the provisions they may contain are governed by the constitutional and statutory laws that apply to municipal incorporations in each of the fifty states.[9] The International City/County Management Association identifies five main forms of community government that structure power and authority: mayor-council, council-manager, commission, town meeting, and representative town meeting.[10] The latter two forms are found only in New England cities.

Table 2.2 shows the distribution of charter types among U.S. cities in 1984 and 2004 with populations of 2,500 or more. The most striking change that occurred during this twenty-year period was the increase in the number of cities that adopted the council-manager form. In 1984, the majority of cities (55.8 percent) had a mayor-council charter, but by 2004 the proportion of cities with this form declined to 43.6 percent. In 1984, just over one-third of cities had a council-manager charter, but twenty years later almost half of all cities (48.7 percent) had this type of charter. In the world of municipal government, this shift represents a virtual sea change in the distribution of structural types. To understand why this change occurred, a brief review of the background of each of the two major types of local government structures is useful.

Outside of New England, the mayor-council form was the original structure for most cities and was patterned after the separation of powers and the checks and balances design of the federal and state governments. In this form, the mayor is the popularly elected chief executive officer (CEO), who may be

Table 2.2.   Frequency of Municipal Government Forms in All U.S. Cities 2,500 and Larger

	1984		2004	
Form	N	Percent	N	Percent
Council-manager	2,290	34.7	3,453	48.7
Mayor-council	3,686	55.8	3,089	43.6
Commission	176	2.7	145	2.0
Town meeting	369	5.6	338	4.8
Representative town meeting	370	5.6	63	.8
Unknown	81	1.2	3	.04
Total	6,603	100	7,091	100

Source: ICMA, "Inside the Year Book: Cumulative Distribution of U.S. Municipalities," in The Municipal Year Book (Washington, D.C.: ICMA, 1984–2004).

empowered to hire and fire department heads, prepare and administer the budget, and sometimes veto (subject to override) the acts of the local legislative body, which is referred to as the council, board, or commission depending on the language of the local charter. Some cities with this form of government may retain the services of a professional administrative officer (CAO) to manage daily government operations. This individual may serve at the pleasure of the mayor and sometimes also with the consent of the town council or board. The typical responsibilities of a city council, most of whose members are usually elected from electoral districts rather than in citywide races, include adopting the budget, passing ordinances, enacting general policy, and exercising oversight of the executive. The political values implicitly emphasized in this form are responsiveness to political constituencies and political leadership.

In the council-manager form, now the most prevalent among all cities, council members historically are elected in "at-large" or citywide nonpartisan contests rather than in partisan, district races. Typically, the council selects the mayor, a position that is largely ceremonial in this form of government. (Often the person who received the largest number of popular votes in the last council race is selected as the mayor.) The council is the municipal governing body that establishes policy and reviews and approves the budget. One of the council's most important responsibilities is to hire a city manager who serves as the city's CEO. The city manager is responsible for the daily management of service operations, preparation and presentation of the city budget, and implementation of the policies adopted by the council. The manager serves as the chief adviser to the council and continues in that position, typically at the pleasure of the council.[11]

The council-manager form emerged as one of the strategies of the urban reform movement, which was itself a product of the Progressive Era in early twentieth-century America. The driving force for municipal reform came from business and professional groups, which wished to curtail the corruption, graft, and excesses of urban bosses and their political machines.[12] Their drive for increased economy and adoption of proven business practices reflected an emphasis on the values of efficiency and managerial competence. Some scholars contend that the reformers' proposed changes in government structure and electoral rules (council-manager form and nonpartisan, at-large elections) were really intended to further diminish the political clout of lower-class citizens.[13] Others suggest that these reforms were meant to revitalize local democracy by strengthening grassroots popular participation and control over government.[14]

Whatever their motivation, most reformers at the time must have considered it impossible to eliminate graft and corruption without freeing city government from partisan politics, represented in its most egregious form by the infamous Tammany organization of New York.[15] This democratic party machine and others like it in some of America's large cities enthusiastically embraced the "honest graft" ethos of Tammany sage George Washington Plunkitt, who best summed it up with the statement: "I seen my opportunities and I took 'em."[16]

Among the study population of small cities (those with populations between 2,500 and 25,000 in 2000 and with either a mayor-council or council-manager government), the most prevalent type of government remains the mayor-council form. Our national survey indicated that about 53 percent of small cities had this type of charter, compared with 46.7 percent that had the council-manager form. As table 2.3 shows, there are substantial differences among cities in the different geographic regions with respect to the predominant form. The majority of the older cities in the Northeast and Midwest have a mayor-council charter, while the majority of more recently incorporated cities in the West and South have council-manager charters. Even though just under half of all small cities have a council-manager form of government, it is important to reiterate that about two-thirds of all city managers (1,801 of 2,796) in the United States are employed by these small communities.[17]

Frederickson, Logan, and Wood argue correctly that a simplistic classification of cities by type of charter fails to capture the nature and pattern of the structural changes that may characterize cities.[18] In their analysis of cities with populations of 10,000 or more, they find a pattern of dynamic change in response to evolving community expectations about what functions government should provide and how local government ought to be structured to provide them.[19] In fact, while many cities adopted the council-manager form in

Table 2.3. Frequency of Governmental Forms in Small Communities by Region, 2000

Region	Mayor-Council Cities		Council-Manager Cities	
	N	Percent	N	Percent
NE	900	32.5	518	21.3
S	748	27.0	830	34.2
MW	935	33.7	638	26.3
W	190	6.8	443	18.2
Totals	2,773	100.0	2,429	100.0
By form	2,773	53.3	2,429	46.7

Source: ICMA, *The Municipal Yearbook* (Washington, D.C.: ICMA, 2000).

the first half of the twentieth century, the second half of the century saw wide-spread adoption by mayor-council cities of some of the more prominent features of "reform" government, most notably a professional executive and a civil service merit system.[20] Simultaneously, many council-manager cities adopted some of the more prominent features of mayor-council government, such as popular election of the mayor and election of at least some council members from districts.[21]

These changes led Frederickson, Johnson, and Wood to suggest that contemporary municipal government structure is best captured by distinguishing among three major forms of local government: "political" (the traditional mayor-council form), "administrative" (the traditional council-manager form), and "adaptive" (a combination of features from the other two types).[22] These scholars conceptualized the three main forces that have influenced the contemporary pattern of structural change and diffusion as drives for "political leadership, political responsiveness, and administrative efficiency."[23] They contend that if the observed patterns of change in municipal structure continue, there will be fewer cities in the "political" and "administrative" categories and more cities in one of the "adaptive" categories. Accordingly, the modal city of the future may likely have a directly elected mayor, a professional city manager or chief administrative officer, some or all council members elected from districts, a civil service merit system, formal bid and purchasing controls, and required external audits.[24]

The empirical analysis by Frederickson, Johnson, and Wood of 1996 data that they obtained from the ICMA and a 1998 survey of a small sample of cities larger than 10,000 population suggested that most cities with one of the two dominant charter forms (between 69 and 71 percent) already have adopted at least some of the features of the other type that qualifies them for placement in one of three "adapted city" types.[25] They estimated that cities in the "political" category comprised between 8 and 16.3 percent of all cities, while "administrative" cities constituted about 14.7 to 21 percent of the total.[26]

To what extent have small U.S. communities emulated the changes observed among larger U.S. cities? Following the conceptual definitions advanced by Frederickson, Johnson, and Wood, we classified the population of small cities into one of the three types according to the following features:

"Political" cities:

- mayor-council charter form
- direct popular election of the mayor
- no chief administrative officer
- most council members elected from districts

"Adapted" cities:

- statutory charter form, either mayor-council or council-manager
- mayor either directly elected or selected by council and may have veto power
- has or likely to have a chief administrative officer
- council elected by district, at-large, or mixed

"Administrative" cities:

- council-manager form
- mayor is selected from among council or has no executive powers
- full-time professional administrator usually called a city manager
- most council members elected at-large

Following these classifications, we compared our findings for small cities with those reported by Frederickson, Johnson, and Wood for larger cities. Even though the data in table 2.4 are cross-sectional, there is evidence that small cities have emulated the pattern of change evidenced among larger cities. When it comes to the diffusion of ideas for structural change, small cities do not appear to have lagged behind their larger counterparts in adopting those structural features that local officials think may advance the values of both efficiency and political responsiveness. Like larger cities, the majority of small communities (55.3 percent) are categorized best as "adaptive" cities. Proportionally, there are about twice as many small cities that remain in the "administrative"

Table 2.4.   **Government Structures in Large and Small U.S. Cities**

Type Structure	Large Cities Survey, 1998*		Small Cities Survey, 2000	
	N	Percent	N	Percent
Political	19	16.3	63	12.4
Adaptive	80	69.0	281	55.3
Administrative	17	14.7	164	32.3
Total	116	100.0	508	100.0

* Described in H. George Fredrickson, Gary Johnson, and Curtis Wood, *The Adapted City: Institutional Dynamics and Structural Change* (Armonk, N.Y.: M. E. Sharpe, 2004).

category compared to larger cities. Conversely, the proportion of small cities in the "political" category is somewhat smaller than for larger cities.

Among the small cities in the "adaptive" category, the majority (73 percent) have a mayor-council form of government. This finding suggests that many small communities with a mayor-council statutory form of government have found it more efficacious and perhaps easier to adapt some of the features of the council-manager form rather than to enact a wholesale change in their type of charter. Compared to larger cities, fewer small cities with council-manager charters adopted the various features of the mayor-council form.

If the distribution of structural features is any indication, it appears that many small local communities with mayor-council charters are keenly concerned about increasing or enhancing the economy, efficiency, and effectiveness of their services. The fiscal pressures experienced by many of these small cities as a result of cuts in state aid or pressures on local services and infrastructure may have been the motivating factors for adoption of some of the features of administrative governments. By comparison, fewer small cities with a council-manager charter appeared to be interested in structural changes that may have promoted the political responsiveness of their government. The findings reported in chapter 3 concerning the political responsiveness of city managers help to explain why this is the case.

In addition to form of government, there are a number of other features of small city governments that together shape and provide the institutional context and dynamics for local policy and decision making. Heretofore, little was known about the various features of small city legislative bodies, chief executives, and the municipal workforce. The portrait of small city governments that emerges from our national survey reflects the diversity of institutional changes adopted by local officials in response to the evolving problems and needs of the citizens.

Table 2.5 reports several of the key attributes of contemporary small city governments. While our findings are consonant with those of Frederickson, Johnson, and Wood that there are fewer examples of either "pure" municipal form, the form of government dichotomy more clearly illustrates the various attributes of and changes adopted by small cities. The mean term for mayors in council-manager cities is somewhat shorter (2.51 years) than the term for mayors in mayor-council cities (3.47 years). More than two-thirds (68 percent) of council-manager cities elect a mayor by direct popular vote who also

Table 2.5. Attributes of Small City Governments by Charter Type, 2000

Feature	Mayor-Council cities		Council-Manager cities	
	N	Percent	N	Percent
Type city charter	268	52.8	240	47.2
Mean years with type charter	101	(n =232)	35	(n = 201)
Mayors				
Mean length of mayor's term of office	3.47	(n = 268)	2.51*	(n = 237)
Mayor elected by popular vote	260	97.0	159	68.0
Mayor elected by council vote	8	3.0	75	32.0*
Mayor's position is full-time	90	34.0	n.a.	n.a.
Mayor's position is part-time	178	66.0	n.a.	n.a.
City has a CAO	135	50.4	n.a.	n.a.
Mayor can hire/fire CAO	34	27.0	n.a.	n.a.
Mayor votes on issues before council	87	32.5	150	64.4*
Mayor has veto power on council actions	151	56.3	46	19.8
Councils				
Mean size of legislative body	5.94	(n = 268)	6.09	(n = 51)
Modal length of council term of office	3.32	(n = 268)	3.34	(n = 240)
Most council members in partisan elections	83	31.0	49	20.4*
Most council members in nonpartisan elections	185	69.0	191	79.6*
Most council members from districts	101	38.0	73	30.8*
Most council members at-large	167	62.0	164	69.2*
City Employees				
Mean size of the municipal workforce	104	(n = 244)	136*	(n = 227)
Mean number of full-time employees	80	(n = 250)	105*	(n = 231)
Mean number of part-time employees	24	(n = 245)	31	(n = 227)
Mean number of full-time municipal employees per capita	207	(n = 250)	151*	(n = 231)
All full- and part-time workers per capita	124	(n =244)	115*	(n = 227)
Have at least some unionized employees	130	49.6	139	57.3*

* Statistically significant difference at the .05 level.
n.a. = not available or not applicable.

has a vote on issues before the council. Only about 20 percent of mayors in council-manager cities have veto power on various council actions. In mayor-council cities, most mayors (56 percent) can veto council actions.

One of the clearest indications of the extent to which small cities with mayor-council charters may be concerned about the values of service efficiency and effectiveness is that over half (50.4 percent) have retained the services of a CAO. Technically, the mayor remains the CEO, but the chief administrative or operating officer is responsible for supervising and directing department heads and managing daily city operations. The CAO serves entirely at the pleasure of the mayor in 27 percent of cities, while mayors share control over the CAO's appointment and retention with council in 72 percent of cities. No doubt the mayors with a CAO need this help since in two-thirds of communities with the mayor-council form, the position of mayor is technically part-time.

The mean size of city councils in the two main charter forms is about six members. The mean length of council members' terms in both forms also is about the same. Most council members in both forms are elected in nonpartisan races but council-manager governments have a slight edge in this respect (79.6 percent versus 69 percent). Most council members in both forms also are elected at-large, rather than in district elections. That there are fewer structural differences between the two charter types underscores the fact that the majority of small cities are classified best as "adaptive" cities.

One distinction that remains apparent between the two charter forms concerns the relative size of the municipal workforce. Since council-manager cities tend to be somewhat larger in terms of population size than mayor-council cities, they have a significantly larger mean number of full-time municipal employees. Consequently, per capita measures of workforce size are better indicators of this local government feature. The per capita measures for just full-time employees and for full- and part-time employees indicate that council-manager cities have significantly *fewer* municipal employees than mayor-council cities. This significant difference reflects an emphasis placed on the value of service economy and efficiency in small council-manager cities.

Nationally, about 46 percent of all local government employees are represented by unions, with the largest numbers usually affiliated with occupations related to education, firefighting, and law enforcement.[27] Small cities that have a council-manager form of government are more likely to have at least some of their employees represented by a union. About 57.3 percent of council-manager cities have at least some of their employees represented by unions, compared with 49.6 percent of their mayor-council counterparts. While the smaller mean size of mayor-council cities might account for part of this difference, we would have expected to find the opposite distribution considering the traditional emphasis on political responsiveness in mayor-council cities. This finding suggests that city managers are more likely to have to engage in collective bargaining activities than their mayoral counterparts.

THE CHIEF EXECUTIVES OF SMALL COMMUNITIES

Overseeing local government operations and providing citizens with services that many of the recipients take for granted is a tough and challenging job. The extent to which a chief executive is able to keep a city running smoothly and efficiently depends on a number of factors, not the least of which are the personal traits, skills, knowledge, and abilities that individual executives bring to the job; the formal powers of the office; and the political environment in which they serve. A number of studies have profiled the career paths, powers, and leadership skills of municipal executives in the nation's larger cities.[28] The results of our national survey of small city CEOs provide a profile of the characteristics of small town leaders and permit analysis of whether any significant differences exist between mayors and city managers with respect to their personal attributes, education, experience, and career paths.

In public administration, we know a lot more about the features of municipal government than we do about the people who serve them. Who are the chief executive officers of small cities? What education and experience do they have? What are their typical career paths to service as a mayor or city manager? How alike or different are contemporary small city mayors and managers? It is particularly important to profile these local officials since analyses in later chapters suggest that there are important distinctions between them, especially with respect to their decision-making processes and the impact they have in promoting a higher level of urban service quality.

Our national survey indicates that the "typical" small town chief executive is white, male, and college-educated and has served an average of seven years as a CEO. Several background factors, however, distinguish mayors and city managers. As table 2.6 shows, women are more likely to be found among the ranks of mayors than city managers. About one in five mayors is female, while only about 7 percent of city managers are female. City managers generally are somewhat younger than their mayoral counterparts. Their average age is forty-eight, while the typical mayor is fifty-five years old.

One of the most distinctive differences between city managers and mayors is their formal educational background. While about three-fourths of mayors have a bachelor's degree, only about one-fourth have some type of graduate

Table 2.6.   Characteristics of Small City Chief Executives, 2000 National Survey

Characteristic	Mayors		City Managers	
	N	Percent	N	Percent
Mean tenure in position (years)	6.78	(266)	7.1	(240)
Mean age	55.0	(262)	48.0*	(240)
Gender:				
Male	217	81.0	224	93.3
Female	51	19.0*	16	6.7
Race:				
White	257	98.0	229	96.2
Nonwhite	5	2.0	9	3.8
Highest formal education:				
Bachelor's or less	197	74.0	90	37.5
Master's or more	69	26.0	150	62.5*
Field of highest degree:				
Public administration	42	21.8	146	64.0*
Business	52	26.9	32	14.0
Engineering	10	5.2	11	4.8
Finance	10	5.2	9	3.9
Other	79	40.9	30	13.2
Party preference:				
Republican	101	38.4	77	32.4
Democrat	100	38.0	50	21.0
Independent	28	10.6	4	1.7
Other or none	34	12.9	107	45.0*
Career path:				
Prior service on council	107	44.4*	2	.8
Manager or assistant manager in same or another city	15	6.2	148	61.9*
Service /employment with other local government department	39	16.2	66	27.6
Private sector business	37	15.4	13	10.4
Private citizen	21	8.7	8	3.3
Education	11	4.6	1	.4
Lawyer	11	4.6	1	.4

* Difference statistically significant at the .05 level.

degree. That the largest proportion of mayors have a degree in a field other than one of those listed suggests that their educational background is quite diverse. By contrast, more than 62 percent of city managers have at least a master's degree. The most common graduate degree field for city managers is public administration; almost two-thirds have graduate degrees in this field.

As one might expect of individuals whose positions are obtained through electoral victory, mayors are more likely than city managers to indicate an overt party preference. About three-fourths (76 percent) of mayors identify with one of the two major national parties, with each party attracting about half of those mayors who expressed a preference. By contrast, just over half (53.4 percent) of city managers indicated a party preference. The majority of these city managers identified with the Republican party.

When it comes to partisanship, however, the most apparent distinction between mayors and city managers is the large proportion of city managers (45 percent) who expressed no party preference whatsoever. Since the ICMA code of ethics urges city managers to refrain from involvement in local election campaigns, managers may prefer to be perceived as nonpartisan, especially when responding to a survey question.[29] However, claiming nonpartisanship status with respect to local elections does not necessarily mean that city managers are apolitical, since our survey indicates that most do in fact have a party preference.

What is the career path for small town mayors and city managers? For mayors, prior service on the local legislative body is the most common springboard to higher elected office. About 44 percent of mayors served previously on the local council. The next most common path to the mayoral office (for about 16.2 percent of mayors) consists of service with a city department, commission, or office. Among this group, the most common connections in order of frequency were with the local planning commission, the police department, and the city clerk's office. For about 15 percent of mayors, their previous position was as a private sector business owner or manager in a local company. Finally, 8.7 percent of mayors indicated that they were private citizens prior to election. The largest proportion of these individuals identified themselves as being retired military officers.

The career paths for city managers are decidedly different. Like their counterparts in larger cities, most city managers in our study (about 62 percent) can be classified as either "ladder climbers" or "single-city careerists."[30] Ladder climbers are individuals hired from another city typically about the same or smaller size, where they worked as an assistant city manager or as the city manager. Single-city careerists are individuals who served previously as an assistant city manager (or in some other capacity) in the same jurisdiction where they are now the city manager. About 28 percent of city managers worked previously in the same city but in another department, most typically in either the finance or budget department. The next most frequent departmental affiliations for city managers were economic development or planning, public works, and the police department.

This profile of small town chief executives indicates distinct differences among mayors and city managers with respect to their education, training, and government experience. While both types of executives may share the same spirit and desire to serve their respective communities, city managers appear to have an edge in terms of their educational preparation and previous experience with municipal service operations.

THE ISSUES THAT CONCERN SMALL CITY CHIEF EXECUTIVES

To ascertain whether differences occurred among chief executives with respect to their perceptions of the significance of problems confronting their communities as they entered the second millennium, the CEOs in the national survey were asked to rank the magnitude of various problems in nine local government policy arenas. A four-point scale of significance was offered in which 1 = "no problem," 2 = "minor problem," 3 = "somewhat significant problem," and 4 = "very significant problem." The mean scores for each problem area and the resulting mean rankings by mayors and city managers and by executives in each of the three types of cities are shown in table 2.7.

Among all small city chief executives, the problem area about which a consensus appears to exist, as least as far as its high level of significance, is the deteriorating condition of and problems with the adequacy of the local transportation system, particularly roads and bridges. It is unknown whether these problems relate to the age, design capacity, safety, or congestion of the local transportation system. However, there is a statistically significant positive correlation between a higher ranking of problems with roads and bridges and the amount by which the city's population grew between 1990 and 2000. Undoubtedly, population growth has exacerbated problems with local transportation systems.

Rounding out the top five most significant problem areas for small cities are economic development, public transportation, education, and water/sewer problems. There is only minor variation in the mean rankings of problems by mayors and city managers and executives in the different types of cities. Uniformity rather than disparity characterizes executive perceptions about the relative significance of problems that confront small cities.

Table 2.7. Rankings of Community Problems by Type of CEO and Type of Government Structure

Problem Area	All CEOs		Mayors		City Managers		"Political" Cities		"Adaptive" Cities		"Administrative" Cities	
	Rank	Mean	Rank	Mean	Rank	Mean	Rank	Mean	Rank	Mean	Rank	Mean
Roads/bridges	1	2.70	2	2.62	1	2.80	2	2.68	1	2.65	1	2.79
Economic development	2	2.50	3	2.57	2	2.42	1	3.00	3	2.46	2	2.38
Transportation	3	2.45	1	2.67	4	2.22	3	2.65	2	2.55	5	2.21
Education	4	2.24	4	2.29	5	2.19	4	2.28	4	2.23	3	2.25
Water/sewer	5	2.22	6	2.19	3	2.25	5	2.14	5	2.22	4	2.23
Housing	6	2.15	5	2.25	6	2.03	6	2.06	6	2.21	6	2.06
Public health	7	1.84	8	1.84	7	1.85	6	2.06	8	1.80	7	1.83
Solid waste	8	1.82	7	1.88	8	1.75	8	1.84	7	1.86	8	1.73
Public safety	9	1.74	9	1.74	9	1.73	9	1.76	9	1.74	9	1.71

These results suggest that many small cities are experiencing problems most closely akin to urban "growing pains." Sustaining an adequate transportation infrastructure and promoting the local economy appear to present the most significant challenges for chief executives. While particular cities may confront urgent and serious issues related to education, utilities, housing, public health, or public safety, the "pre-9/11" perceptions of chief executives were clearly dominated by concerns about local transportation and economic development.

SUMMARY

Overall, the residents of America's small towns are more socially homogeneous than the nation as a whole, although the immigration of Hispanics is beginning to change the character of many small communities. Most residents of small communities have not yet attained a college degree in the same proportion as the rest of the country, but they do not lag far behind national averages in terms of either income, high school graduation, or the educational quality of their public schools.

Most small cities experienced significant population growth between 1990 and 2000. The majority of small cities are now located within the boundaries of either a micropolitan or metropolitan statistical area. Significant change also has occurred with respect to the structural features of municipalities. Like their larger counterparts, many small cities have adopted various structural features that make a simple dichotomy between forms of government much less descriptive and accurate. The majority of small communities are now best described as having an "adaptive" governmental structure.

Several characteristics distinguish mayors and city managers. Each type of chief executive has followed a distinctly different educational and employment path to his or her respective positions of leadership. However, a consensus appears to exist among chief executives concerning the significance of the transportation infrastructure and economic development problems that confront their cities. The ways in which the distinguishing characteristics of mayors and city managers play out in their decision-making processes and impact on local services are explored in subsequent chapters.

NOTES

1. *Federal Register* 65, no. 249 (December 27, 2000).
2. *Federal Register* 65, no. 249, 82238.
3. *Federal Register* 65, no. 249, 82238.

4. Bryan D. Stumpf, *Small Towns Facing Rapid Growth*, Arizona State University, 1999, at www.asu.edu/caed/proceedings99 (accessed July 19, 2004).

5. The Education Achievement index is a rating of the school's performance on a scale of 1 to 10, where a 10 is best. This index is purportedly based on state and national achievement tests and the percentage of students who continue to college. See Bert Sperling, *Best Places*, 2002, at www.bestplaces.net/city/ccompare.aspx (accessed July 9, 2004). Sources for the other variables included in table 2.1 are U.S. Census Bureau, "1990 Summary Tape File 1 (STF 1)," 2000, at factfinder.census.gov/servlet/ (accessed July 12, 2004); U.S. Census Bureau, "Summary File 1C," 2000, at factfinder.census .gov/servlet/ (accessed July 12, 2004); and U.S. Census Bureau, "Summary File 3," 2000, at factfinder.census.gov/servlet/ (accessed July 12, 2004).

6. See David R. Morgan and Robert E. England, *Managing Urban America* (New York: Chatham House, 1999); Susan Welch and Timothy Bledsoe, *Urban Reform and Consequences* (Chicago: University of Chicago Press, 1988); R. Kent Weaver and Bert A. Rockman, *Do Institutions Matter? Government Capabilities in the United States and Abroad* (Washington, D.C.: Brookings Institution, 1993); James H. Svara, *Official Leadership in the City: Patterns of Conflict and Cooperation* (Oxford: Oxford University Press, 1990); and Robert L. Lineberry and Edmond P. Fowler, "Reformism and Public Policies in American Cities," *American Political Science Review* 61, no. 3 (1967): 701–16.

7. Harold D. Lasswell, *Politics: Who Gets What, When, and How?* (New York: McGraw-Hill, 1936).

8. Deborah A. Stone, *Policy Paradox and Political Reason* (Glenview, Ill.: Scott Foresman, 1988).

9. The U.S. Constitution makes no mention of local government. The creation of a municipality and the types of permissible city charters are governed by the constitutional and statutory provisions of each state. These laws invariably address the powers granted or denied to cities. Most states also provide for an optional method for municipal incorporation called "home-rule." Under the provisions of home-rule, cities are given the authority to draft, adopt, and amend their own charters and governmental structure. Home-rule cities are presumed to possess all necessary governmental power to act except as restricted by state statutes. On the other hand, a non–home-rule city can exercise only those powers explicitly or implicitly granted to them by state laws (also called enabling legislation). In these cases, a special legislative act may be required for a city to engage in an activity not specifically or implicitly authorized by state law. An example might be a city that wishes to establish an environmental court to prosecute cases of illegal dumping or littering when such authority is not explicitly granted to municipal governments under a state's statutes. See Thomas C. Marks Jr. and John F. Cooper, *State Constitutional Law* (St. Paul, Minn.: West Publishing, 1988).

10. International City/County Management Association, *The Municipal Year Book*, 21 vols. (Washington, D.C.: ICMA Press, 1984–2004).

11. Most city managers serve without a guaranteed term or tenure; however, almost 80 percent of managers have employment agreements that set the terms and conditions

of employment and separation and often contain guidelines for performance evaluation. See William H. Hansell Jr., *Evolution and Change Characterize Council-Manager Government* (Washington, D.C.: ICMA Press, 2004), at www2.icma.org/main/1did=14265 &hsid=1&ssid1=44&ssis2=79&ssid3=79 (accessed October 25, 2004).

12. Samuel P. Hays, "The Politics of Reform in Municipal Government in the Progressive Era," *Pacific Northwest Quarterly* 55 (October 1964): 157–89; and Dennis R. Judd, *The Politics of American Cities: Private Power and Public Policy* (Glenview, Ill.: Scott Foresman, 1988).

13. Judd, *Politics of American Cities*.

14. Edward C. Banfield and James Q. Wilson, *City Politics* (New York: Vintage Press, 1963).

15. Morgan and England, *Managing Urban America*.

16. William L. Riordon, *Plunkitt of Tammany Hall: A Series of Very Plain Talks on Very Practical Politics* (Boston: St. Martin's, 1994), 49.

17. The figure of three-quarters was computed from International City/County Management Association, *The Municipal Yearbook* (Washington, D.C.: ICMA Press, 2000), xi, table 2.

18. H. George Frederickson, Brett Logan, and Curtis Wood, "Municipal Reform in Mayor-Council Cities: A Well-Kept Secret," *State and Local Government Review* 35, no. 1 (2003): 7–14; and H. George Frederickson, Gary A. Johnson, and Curtis Wood, *The Adapted City: Institutional Dynamics and Structural Change* (Armonk, N.Y.: M. E. Sharpe, 2004).

19. Frederickson et al., *The Adapted City*.

20. Tari Renner and Victor S. DeSantis, "Municipal Form of Government: Issues and Trends," in *The Municipal Yearbook*, 30–41 (Washington, D.C.: ICMA Press, 1998).

21. Frederickson et al., *The Adapted City*; Ruth Hoogland DeHoog and Gordon P. Whitaker, "Political Conflict or Professional Advancement: Alternative Explanations for City Manager Turnover." *Journal of Urban Affairs*, 12, no. 4 (1990): 361–77.

22. Frederickson et al., *The Adapted City*.

23. Frederickson et al., *The Adapted City*, 329.

24. Frederickson et al., *The Adapted City*.

25. Frederickson et al., *The Adapted City*.

26. Frederickson et al., *The Adapted City*, 104–10.

27. Bureau of Labor Statistics news release, January 21, 2004, at ftp://ftp.bls .gov/pub/news.release/History/union2.01212004 (accessed October 26, 2004).

28. See Douglas J. Watson and Wendy L. Hassett, "Career Paths in America's Largest Council-Manager Cities," *Public Administration Review* 64, no. 2 (2004): 192–99; Richard C. Feiock and Christopher Stream, "Explaining the Tenure of Local Government Managers," *Journal of Public Administration Research and Theory* 8, no. 1 (1998): 117–31; Glenn Abney and Thomas P. Lauth, *The Politics of State and City Administration* (Albany: University of New York Press, 1986); Larry D. Terry, *Leadership of Public Bureaucracies: The Administrator as Conservator* (Thousand Oaks, Calif.: Sage, 1995); Leonard I. Ruchelman, *Big City Mayors: The Crisis in Urban Politics* (Bloomington: Indiana University Press, 1969); Susan E. Clarke and Gary Gaile,

The Work of Cities (Minneapolis: University of Minnesota Press, 1998); and James R. Bowers and Wilbur C. Rich, *Governing Middle-Sized Cities: Studies in Mayoral Leadership* (Boulder, Colo.: Rienner, 2000).

29. International City/County Management Association, *Code of Ethics*, July 2004, at www2.icma.org/main/bc.asp?bcid=40&hsid=1&ssid1=17&ssid2=24 (accessed July 20, 2004).

30. Watson and Hassett, "Career Paths," 192–99.

3

Executive Behavior and Decision Making

How do small city chief executives allocate their time and balance the political and administrative dimensions of their jobs? To what extent are they involved in decisions related to the mission, policy, administrative, and management dimensions of the governmental process? With whom do they consult in making these decisions, and to what extent are these decisions influenced by different stakeholders in the community? What implications do these patterns of decision making have for the relative responsiveness of mayors and city managers to different local interests and constituencies? This chapter presents evidence that there are several important behavioral differences among these two types of executives, but responsiveness to community interests is not among them.

Public administration practitioners and scholars recognize that politics and administration are inextricably linked in the policy decision-making process in local government. The idea that there ever was or even should be a dichotomy between them has been convincingly refuted by numerous scholars.[1] Recognizing that professional managers are not insulated from the politics of local decision making, researchers have examined the nature of the relationship between elected and appointed officials with the aim of trying to ascertain whether unelected public managers are sufficiently responsive and accountable to elected representatives and other stakeholders in the community. The quest to define "the appropriate relationship between elected and appointed officials" has engendered much debate about what level of discretion is appropriate for unelected officials in a democratic government.[2]

While most scholars agree that institutional arrangements affect, at least on the margin, the nature of local policies and the responsiveness of executive officials, no consensus exists about the precise impact of those effects and whether they auger good or ill for the quality of local democratic governance. Political scientists such as Theodore Lowi have asserted, for example, that professional administrators can be expected to acquire power unfettered by the constraints that limit their elected counterparts.[3] This suggests that professional administrators are more susceptible to "mission creep." Conversely, the implication is that elected officials are more likely to be responsive to various community interests because their actions can be validated or rejected by citizens at the ballot box. Other scholars have suggested that professional managers *should* play a very active role in the policy-making process because their insight, knowledge, and expertise can contribute to solutions for complex problems.[4] What is clear to many practicing city managers is that they ignore the political dimension of their jobs at their own peril. As one long-time city management consultant observed, the courageous and effective city manager is one who "seeks and listens to input from the council . . . challenges city processes to be more responsive to community stakeholders . . . [and] is driven by what is best for the city over personal agenda or gain."[5]

As explained in chapter 2, the structure of local government provides an important context for the interaction of local executives and other community interests in the policy-making process. One aspect of this interaction about which little is known empirically is whether there are any significant differences in the decision-making processes of mayors and city managers that suggest whether one type of executive might be more or less responsive to community stakeholders. Svara explains that "the behavior of officials is crucial to fashioning the governmental process for better or worse."[6] Accordingly, questions about how mayors and city managers view their roles in the four dimensions of the governmental process (mission, policy, administration, and management) and how they go about making decisions on issues related to these dimensions have consequences that merit further examination. By comparing how mayors and city managers work within and around the constraints of their governmental structure, it may be possible to better discern how each type of executive deals with the demands of his or her job and balances the political and administrative aspects of his or her position.

Svara, as well as Frederickson, Logan, and Wood, have suggested that important differences may exist among mayor-council cities that have an appointed CAO and those that do not have a CAO.[7] This analysis captures differences by examining mayoral behavior among cities with and without CAOs and compares them to city managers in council-manager cities. Also examined are whether any differences in executive behavior appear among the three main types of local government structures (political, adaptive, and professional). This dual approach facilitates detection of behavioral differences that may occur among the two types of executives and between executives who serve in different types of government structures.

Our focus in this chapter is how local chief executives allocate their time among activities related to policy and administration and how contemporary chief executives' role emphases compare to previous research findings. Svara's framework of the governmental process is used to compare how mayors and city managers perceive their level of involvement in activities related to the mission, policy, administration, and management of their locality.[8] Next, we examine a particularly important facet of decision making by mayors and city managers that pertains to their patterns of consultation in making decisions about issues related to local services and programs. This chapter concludes with an analysis of how chief executives perceive their decisions to be influenced or shaped specifically by the involvement of community interest groups.

These comparisons seek to answer several specific questions that should inform subsequent analyses of how contemporary local executives "mix" or balance the political and administrative dimensions of their jobs. For instance, are there differences in how contemporary mayors and city managers allocate their time and emphasize particular roles? Have these role emphases changed over time? Do mayors and city managers differ in the extent to which they perceive their level of involvement in the dimensions of the governmental process? Do mayors and city managers exhibit different patterns of consultation in making decisions? To what extent do local chief executives perceive that local interest groups shape or influence their decisions? Finally, what are the implications of these findings for the larger question of and continuing debate about executive responsiveness, structural features, and how different chief executives can balance local politics and administration?

ROLE EMPHASES AND TIME ALLOCATION
AMONG CHIEF EXECUTIVES

In 1965, Deil Wright examined how city managers in forty-five cities with populations larger than 100,000 allocated their time among different roles. His work was the first to document the extent to which city managers were involved in activities that ranged beyond those related to management per se (staffing, budgeting, coordination, supervision, and evaluation). Wright found that city managers played a significant policy role in local government including activities related to control over the council's agenda, policy initiation, and policy formulation.[9] In 1985 Newell and Ammons conducted a survey of fifty-two city managers and twenty-six mayors in cities with more than 50,000 people.[10] They found that city managers devoted significantly more time than mayors to activities related to policy and management roles.

While there is some ambiguity in the range of activities that could be included under the broad umbrellas of policy and management, the descriptions of such activities employed by Newell and Ammons were followed as closely as possible in the current study.[11] In the national survey, respondents were offered examples of the kinds of activities related to a policy role and a management role and were asked to estimate the amount of time they devoted to each in 1999. The types of policy activities included proposing policy, developing policy, and formulating budget proposals. The types of management activities included making decisions related to staffing, policy implementation, and coordinating departments.

Small city chief executives estimated the percentage of time that they devoted to activities related to a "policy role" and a "management role." Table 3.1 compares the mean proportions of time that these executives devoted to activities in each of these roles and also shows the earlier findings by Newell and Ammons for chief executives of large cities. The columns for "all mayors" and "city managers" in small cities provide the relevant figures to compare with the Newell and Ammons data.

Overall, these findings indicate that small city chief executives, like their counterparts in large cities from an earlier era, spend the largest proportion of their time on activities related to their management role. In both surveys however, city managers spend a significantly larger proportion of their time on both management *and* policy activities than do mayors. This finding indicates that professional city managers are more extensively engaged in these two important functions regardless of city size.

Compared to their counterparts in large cities, managers of small cities allocate somewhat more time to management activities (56 versus 50 percent).

Table 3.1.   Executive Time Allocations Among Policy and Management Roles

Role	Newell & Ammons (1985)*		All Mayors	Mayors No CAO	Mayors with CAO	City Managers
	Mayors	City Managers	Mayors	No CAO	CAO	Managers
Policy	25.6	32.2	26.25	23.67	28.78	30.56
Management	44.2	50.8	36.04	43.10	29.14	56.10**
N	71	142	267	132	135	240

* Published in Charldean Newell and David N. Ammons, "Role Emphases of City Managers and Other Municipal Executives," in *Ideal and Practice in Council-Manager Government*, ed. H. George Fredrickson, 97–107 (Washington, D.C.: ICMA Press, 1995).
** Statistically significant difference at the .05 level between mayors without a CAO and city managers.

This finding is not surprising considering that small city managers typically do not have the same level of staff support as that enjoyed by managers in large cities. Consequently, the typical small city manager spends the majority of his or her professional time on management activities and about one-third on the policy role.

Among all small city chief executives, mayors with no CAO allocated less time to their policy role than did mayors who had the services of a CAO. However, mayors with a CAO spent almost as much time on policy matters as did city managers. This finding suggests that having the services of a professional administrator makes a difference in terms of how much time a mayor is able to devote to local policy issues. Mayors who have a CAO to manage daily government operations appear to benefit by being able to spend more time on policy matters.

What these patterns of time allocation suggest is that the type of chief executive a city has matters a lot more than city size in terms of understanding how much time a chief executive allocates to local policy and management challenges. Our findings indicate that city managers devote a larger proportion of their time to policy matters compared to mayors without a CAO and a much larger proportion of their time to management activities compared to mayors with or without a CAO.

That mayors with a CAO and city managers devote about the same proportion of their time to proposing and developing policy suggests that both types of executives equally value the importance of developing policies to address community needs and issues. Whether this level of executive policy involvement is "optimal" for democratic governance is problematic, but it certainly does not suggest that city managers are bent on dominating local policy making, at least in terms of how they allocate their time in comparison to mayors.

Do the structural features of a local government affect how small city chief executives allocate their time? Figure 3.1 illustrates time allocations among the chief executives in each of the three basic municipal structures. The chief executives of "political" cities consisted of sixty-three mayors who did not have the services of a CAO. In "adaptive" cities, the CEOs consisted of 70 mayors without a CAO, 135 mayors with a CAO, and 76 city managers. All of the 164 CEOs in "administrative" cities were city managers.

Figure 3.1 indicates that structure matters with respect to how chief executives allocate their time among their policy and management roles. The chief executives in political and adaptive cities devote about the same amount of their time to policy-related activities, but the mayors in political cities spend more time on management activities than executives in adaptive cities. However, the city managers in administrative cities spend a statistically larger proportion of

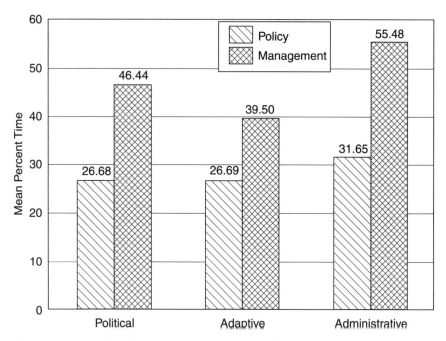

Figure 3.1. Time Allocations Among Small City CEOs by Type of Government Structure

their time on both policy and management issues than executives in either of the other two government structures.

That city managers in "administrative" cities allocate significantly more time to both policy and management roles suggests that these executives may operate under a different set of performance expectations than their counterparts in other structures. If city managers in administrative cities are held more directly accountable for results, perhaps these executives feel compelled to devote more attention to both policy and management issues. Conversely, the executives in political and adaptive cities may operate in political environments where responsibility for policy-related activities is more diffuse and shared, which may account for the smaller proportion of time that executives allocate to this role. On the other hand, there may be less attention given to policy and management issues by executives in these cities.

How chief executives allocate their time is just one indicator of the value they place on their different roles and the need to emphasize a particular role within the structural constraints and expectations of the locality. The next section examines how the different types of executives perceive the *extent* of their involvement in the dimensions of the governmental process.

EXECUTIVE INVOLVEMENT IN THE GOVERNMENTAL PROCESS

Svara's model offers an explicit framework for comparing how mayors and city managers are involved in specific activities related to the mission, policy, administration, and management dimensions of the governmental process.[12] Mayors and city managers estimated the extent of their involvement in a number of different activities that were later grouped with one of the four dimensions of the governmental process. The respondents did not have category labels to identify a particular activity with a dimension. A four-point scale was used to ascertain executives' level of involvement in different activities. Respondents were asked to indicate whether they had "1 = no involvement," "2 = low involvement," "3 = moderate involvement," or "4 = high involvement" in various activities. Later, these activities were grouped with the mission, policy, administration, or management dimensions.

Mission involvement was measured by a survey question that asked about the extent to which the respondent was involved in the development of the municipality's goals and mission. Policy involvement was measured by a mean score computed from responses to three questions that asked respondents to indicate their level of involvement in developing policies, proposing local policies, and formulating budget proposals, respectively. Involvement in administration was measured by computing the mean score from responses to three questions that asked respondents to indicate their level of involvement in activities such as supervising policy implementation, coordinating departmental staff, and reviewing decision recommendations. Management involvement was measured by computing a mean score based on responses from three questions that asked respondents to indicate their level of involvement in activities such as hiring or firing staff, managing service contracts, and reviewing budget issues.

The extent to which the different types of small town chief executives perceive their level of involvement in each of the four dimensions of the governmental process is shown in table 3.2. As a group, chief executives generally perceived themselves to be more extensively involved in decisions related to mission and policy activities than in administrative and management activities. For each type of executive, the perceived level of involvement is highest for decisions related to mission activities but diminishes for each of the subsequent dimensions of the governmental process.

However, there are distinct differences among the types of executives. Mayors with no CAO have higher mean levels of perceived involvement in each activity compared to mayors who have a CAO. City managers have statistically higher levels of perceived involvement in decisions related to *each* of the dimensions of the governmental process than either of the two groups

Table 3.2. Executive Involvement in the Dimensions of the Governmental Process

Dimension	Mayors, no CAO	Mayors with CAO	City Managers
Mission	3.36	3.28	3.59*
Policy	2.60	2.43	2.80*
Administration	2.54	2.23	2.75*
Management	2.47	2.21	2.63*
Total Means	2.74	2.53	2.94*

* Statistically significant difference at the .05 level.

of mayors. Although the previous analysis of time allocation indicated little difference between mayors served by a CAO and city managers in terms of the time each typically allocated to the policy role, city managers had an overall level of perceived involvement in each dimension that was more extensive than other executives. In other words, chief executives may spend comparable amounts of time dealing with policy issues, but the extent of their perceived level of involvement in those issues as well as the other dimensions of the governmental process is quite different.

Figure 3.2 shows how executives in the three local government structures perceived their level of involvement in the four dimensions of the governmental process. An analysis of means indicates that structure attenuates the magnitude of the differences in the perceived level of involvement, but executives in administrative cities still have statistically higher levels of perceived involvement compared to executives in political and adaptive cities. This finding indicates that different forms of government have differing patterns of executive involvement in the decisions in each of the dimensions of the governmental process. That city managers in administrative cities have a more extensive level of involvement does not mean that they operate outside a framework of political control or that their arena for decision making is more circumscribed than for executives in other structures.[13] A more compelling question may be, who is watching "the policy store" in cities that lack a professional city manager?

Why do the perceptions of the level of involvement in the dimensions of the governmental process differ for city managers and mayors and for executives in the three forms of government? Svara's typology of leadership for mayors suggests that there may be fewer mayors who pursue activist "reformer" or "innovator" roles and more mayors who assume a "figurehead," "caretaker," or "broker" role.[14] Yates suggested that over time, mayors are more likely to become "caretakers" as other options are closed off and that sustaining a more activist role may generate more conflict than the mayor is capable of resolv-

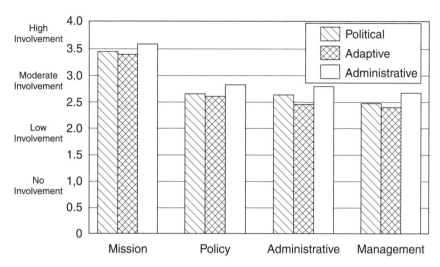

Figure 3.2. Executive Involvement in the Dimensions of the Governmental Process by City Structure

ing.[15] To partially test this assertion, mean scores for mayoral involvement were analyzed to ascertain whether they were related to length of tenure. (The mean tenure for both mayors and city managers was about seven years.) A rough correspondence was assumed to exist between involvement score quartiles and Svara's four descriptive leadership roles. However, no statistically significant relationships occurred between mean involvement scores for mayors and their length of tenure.

An alternative explanation for the difference in reported involvement by mayors and city managers in the four dimensions of the governmental process may relate more particularly to the process that the different executives employ to make decisions about local government services and programs. Following the work of Svara, Ferman, and Feiock and Clingermayer, we hypothesized that mayors and city managers may have different patterns of consultation in terms of the sources from which they are likely to seek advice and input in the process of reaching a decision that concerns local services and programs.[16] If city managers consult with and seek to include a broader array of stakeholders in their decision-making process than do mayors, then perhaps this might help to explain why their perceptions differ in terms of their relative level of involvement in activities related to the dimensions of the governmental process.

PATTERNS OF CONSULTATION IN DECISION
MAKING BY EXECUTIVES

With whom do municipal executives consult in making decisions about issues in local services and programs? Do any significant differences emerge in the patterns of consultation among mayors, mayors with a CAO and city managers, or executives in different forms of city government? To answer these questions, local executives were asked: "With whom do you usually consult in making decisions in each of the following areas?" Respondents were asked to indicate whether they usually consulted with the city council, department heads, the public, or private consultants in making decisions about issues related to the seven local services listed in table 3.3. Respondents could circle any or all groups that they consulted for each service area. Mean scores indicate the extent to which different executives consulted various stakeholders in making executive decisions about the seven services. Responses were coded "1 = yes" and "2 = no," so a lower mean value indicates that the executive was more likely to consult a particular stakeholder.

The pattern of consultation evident in table 3.3 indicates that municipal executives generally consulted with the council, department heads, the public, and then private consultants in order of frequency in making decisions about local services. However, differences occurred in the frequency with which mayors and city managers reported that they consulted with each of these groups. While there were no significant differences in consultation scores among mayors with or without a CAO, the consultation pattern for city managers indicated that they were much more likely than other executives to seek input from and participation by the council, department heads, and the public before they make decisions about local services and programs. The consultation scores for city managers are statistically different than those for mayors for almost all services in two of the four groups (council and department heads). City managers' consultation scores with the public are statistically different for two services (solid waste and parks and recreation).

City managers appear to be more likely than mayors to consult with key stakeholders before they reach a decision that affects a local service or project. Perhaps this broader and apparently more consistent pattern of outreach helps to explain why city managers have a higher perceived level of involvement in the activities related to the four dimensions of the governmental process. Analysis of consultation means and involvement scores on the mission and policy dimensions of the governmental process were modestly correlated at a statistically significant level for consultation with department heads (–.163) and with the public (–.112) in executives' decision process. In other words, those executives who usually consulted with the department

Table 3.3. Patterns of Consultation in Decision Making Among Small City Executives

Service/Program	Council			Department Heads			Public			Consultants		
	Mayor	Mayor with CAO	City Manager	Mayor	Mayor with CAO	City Manager	Mayor	Mayor with CAO	City Manager	Mayor	Mayor with CAO	City Manager
Education	1.55	1.42	1.27*	1.61	1.73	1.59	1.59	1.52	1.56	1.76	1.84	1.84
Economic Development	1.33	1.25	1.10*	1.59	1.55	1.36*	1.64	1.61	1.56	1.47	1.50	1.50
Public Safety	1.34	1.29	1.20*	1.27	1.19	1.15*	1.75	1.66	1.64	1.90	1.89	1.85
Transportation	1.47	1.42	1.24*	1.62	1.64	1.44*	1.60	1.48	1.51	1.72	1.75	1.67
Solid Waste Disposal	1.36	1.31	1.27	1.32	1.36	1.22*	1.79	1.77	1.66*	1.74	1.76	1.65
Parks and Recreation	1.31	1.28	1.24	1.26	1.20	1.09*	1.62	1.58	1.44*	1.77	1.79	1.64*
Public Housing	1.47	1.44	1.22*	1.66	1.75	1.58*	1.60	1.59	1.56	1.59	1.69	1.68
Grand Means	1.43	1.34	1.22*	1.51	1.52	1.36*	1.64	1.57	1.55	1.70	1.73	1.68

* Statistically significant difference for city managers at the .05 level.

heads and the public before making decisions on services also had a higher mean score on the level of perceived involvement in the activities related to the mission and policy dimensions of the governmental process.

Differences also occurred among executives in the three forms of local government with respect to their pattern of consultation with various stakeholders. The findings indicated that city managers in administrative cities were statistically more likely to consult with the city council before making decisions related to all service areas except parks and recreation and solid waste. In making decisions about parks and recreation, city managers in administrative cities were much more likely to consult department heads, the public, and professional consultants than were executives in other forms of government.

Svara's research on large cities led him to conclude that "leadership is and should be collective in the council-manager form" and that "executive mayors need to rely less on power and confrontation and more on inclusive leadership."[17] The findings for small city executives suggest that city managers recognize the value of outreach and forging partnerships among government and community actors to reach decisions about community services and programs. Svara's advice for big city mayors seems equally applicable to their small city counterparts: They would do well to consider how to more effectively mobilize official and popular opinion in their decision-making process.

While differences exist in the patterns of decision consultation among local executives, these do not necessarily capture the extent to which their decisions actually may be shaped by the feedback received from the members of the consulted groups. Whether differences occur in how executives perceive their decisions on local services and programs to be shaped by members of community interest groups is explored next.

THE INFLUENCE OF LOCAL INTEREST GROUPS ON EXECUTIVE DECISIONS

Some scholars have suggested that "reformed" governments are "somewhat resistant to interest group influence" while others hold a contrary view.[18] Other research suggests that interest groups have become extensively involved in local policy making.[19] However, Abney and Lauth's observation is still applicable: "the truth is that not much is known about how local interest groups influence local government policy."[20] It is appropriate therefore to examine how mayors and city managers think local interest groups influence their decisions.

Chief executives were asked to rate the level of influence that any local interest groups have on their decisions on issues related to several types of

Table 3.4. Executives' Perceptions of Interest Group Influence on Decisions

Service Area	Mayors no CAO	Mayors w/ CAO	City Manager	Service Means
Education	2.52	2.45	2.32	2.41
Economic Development	2.95	2.82	2.84	2.86
Public Safety	2.63	2.61	2.70	2.66
Transportation	1.90	1.86	1.77	1.83
Solid Waste Disposal	2.46	2.30	2.35	2.36
Parks and Recreation	2.93	2.91	2.87	2.89
Public Housing	2.02*	1.90	1.80	1.88
Grand Means	2.48	2.41	2.37	2.41

local government services. This self-report measure is considered to be one indicator of the relative responsiveness of executives to an important segment of community stakeholders.[21] The response choices (coded 1 through 4) were "no influence," "minor influence," "moderate influence," and "major influence." The executives' mean scores for level of interest group influence on their decisions in the seven service areas are reported in table 3.4.

Overall, municipal executives perceived that members of interest groups have between a minor and a moderate influence on the decisions they make about these seven local services or programs. The services for which executives report that interest groups have the most influence on their decisions are parks and recreation, economic development, and public safety. However, the analysis of means indicated that there were virtually *no* statistically significant differences in how mayors and city managers rated the perceived level of influence that interest groups had in shaping their decisions on these local services. The only exception was one relationship for mayors with no CAO, whose mean score for the influence of public housing interests was statistically higher than the mean scores for the other executives.

A comparison of the mean influence scores among executives in the three municipal government forms yielded similar findings. Executives in all three government structures rated interest groups for parks and recreation, economic development, and public safety as having the most influence on their decisions, but there was no statistically significant difference in how executives rated the influence of community stakeholders.

Based on previous research, one might expect popularly elected chief executives to report a higher perceived level of influence of interest groups on their decisions about local service issues or that city managers might be influenced more by local business interests who have a particular stake in local economic development.[22] That virtually no significant differences emerged between mayors and city managers or among executives in different municipal forms suggests that local interest group members are *equally* likely to influence or shape executive decisions regardless of the type of chief executive in their community. Consequently, these findings indicate that appointed city managers are no less responsive to community stakeholders than are popularly elected mayors.

SUMMARY

City managers as a group, and particularly those in administrative cities, allocate a significantly larger proportion of their time to activities related to their mission and policy roles than do other executives. City managers in small communities spend a lot more time on management functions than do their counterparts in larger cities, which is attributed mainly to having fewer support staff. City managers in this study also have a higher level of perceived involvement in each of the four dimensions of the governmental process. However, this finding does not signify a desire by professional city managers to dominate the local decision process or limit the involvement of other stakeholders.

City managers actually exhibit a distinctly broader and more inclusive pattern of consultation with the council, department heads, and the public in the process of making decisions about local services. In other words, city managers are more likely than mayors or executives in adaptive cities to consult with more local stakeholders as part of their decision process involving issues related to community services. That no important or significant differences exist in how city managers and other chief executives perceive their decisions to be influenced by community interest groups with a stake in seven service policy arenas confirms that there is nothing sinister about professional managers spending more time on or being more involved in local mission or policy issues. Their engagement in each of the dimensions of the governmental process is simply more extensive because their pattern of consultation with other stakeholders is broader and more inclusive.

City managers regularly face the charge that they are "too powerful." This analysis confirms that city managers are indeed more extensively involved in all of the dimensions of the governmental process, including activities related to mission and policy, that one might presume to be the primary domain of elected officials. City managers appear to temper their more extensive involvement in these activities by engaging in a more inclusive pattern of consultation in the process of making decisions that may help to insulate them from potential charges that they are too powerful. We speculate that elected officials in adaptive and particularly administrative cities may tolerate or even expect their city manager to be extensively involved in local mission and policy activities as long as the manager is not or does not appear to be self-serving. Perhaps the observed pattern of more extensive consultation by city managers is just one of the most apparent strategies used to deflect local critics.

Svara observed that the mayor-council form experiences more conflict while the council-manager governments are typically more cooperative.[23] The different patterns of consultation by mayors and city managers in small cities appear to support this observation. At least in terms of their decision process, city managers appear more inclined to practice the politics of cooperation by including a broader array of groups in their decision process, while mayors are inclined to consult less often and with fewer groups. While the narrower and less frequent consultation pattern exhibited by mayors in making decisions does not necessarily equate with more conflict, it seems reasonable to presume that it has this potential.

The different approaches to decision making exhibited by mayors and city managers do not *necessarily* mean that one approach is superior to the other. A conflictive or cooperative decision process may still yield a comparable level of impact that local stakeholders have on the actual decisions reached by executives. One thing, however, is quite clear: Small town mayors, by virtue of being popularly elected, have no advantage over professional city managers with respect to their level of responsiveness to community interests. What city managers bring to the office of chief executive is a more extensive level of involvement and engagement in community mission, policy, administrative, and management activities and a level of receptivity to local interests that is no different from that of an elected executive.

What then are some of the impacts that attend this higher level of executive engagement by city managers in managing small cities? Are there measurable consequences of the professional values that city managers emphasize as chief executives? In other words, does it make any substantive difference whether a small city has an elected or appointed chief executive in the contemporary small municipality? As America's small towns become increasingly popular places in which to live and raise families, it is important for citizens to understand what, if any, benefits accrue from having city services professionally managed. The next chapter describes the implications of having a professional manager that pertain to the level of input service quality provided by the community.

NOTES

1. See Karl L. Bosworth, "The Manager Is a Politician," *Public Administration Review* 18, no. 3 (1958): 216–22; Glenn Abney and Thomas P. Lauth, *The Politics of*

State and City Administration (Albany: State University of New York, 1986); Lawrence J. O'Toole, "Doctrines and Developments: Separation of Powers, the Politics-Administration Dichotomy, and the Rise of the Administrative State," *Public Administration Review* 47, no. 1 (1987): 17–25; Robert S. Montjoy and Douglas J. Watson, "A Case for Reinterpreted Dichotomy of Politics and Administration as a Professional Standard in Council-Manager Government," *Public Administration Review* 55, no. 3 (1995): 231–39; Charldean Newell and David N. Ammons, "Role Emphases of City Managers and Other Municipal Executives," in *Ideal and Practice in Council-Manager Government*, ed. H. George Frederickson, 97–107 (Washington, D.C.: ICMA Press, 1995); Robert T. Golembiewski and Gerald T. Gabris, "Today's City Managers: A Legacy of Success-Becoming-Failure," *Public Administration Review* 54, no. 6 (1994): 525–30; James H. Svara, "The Politics-Administration Dichotomy Model as Aberration," *Public Administration Review* 58, no. 1 (1998): 51–58; James H. Svara, "The Shifting Boundary Between Elected Officials and City Managers in Large Council-Manager Cities," *Public Administration Review* 59, no. 1 (1999a): 44–53; James H. Svara, "Complementarily of Politics and Administration as a Legitimate Alternative to the Dichotomy Model," *Administration and Society* 30, no. 6 (1999b): 676–705; and James H. Svara, "The Myth of the Dichotomy: Complementarily of Politics and Administration in the Past and Future of Public Administration," *Public Administration Review* 61, no. 2 (2001): 176–83. This chapter is a substantially revised version of an article on the same topic published by French and Folz, "Executive Behavior and Decision Making in Small U.S. Cities," *American Public Administration Review* 34, no. 1 (2004): 52–66.

2. Delmer D. Dunn and Jerome S. Legge Jr., "Politics and Administration in U.S. Local Governments," *Journal of Public Administration Research and Theory* 12, no. 3 (2002): 401–22.

3. Theodore J. Lowi, "Legitimizing Public Administration," *Public Administration Review* 53, no. 3 (1993): 261–64; and Theodore J. Lowi, "Lowi Responds," *Public Administration Review* 55, no. 5 (1995): 490–94.

4. See Lawrence Keller and Michael W. Spicer, "Political Science and Public Administration: A Necessary Cleft?" *Public Administration Review* 57, no. 3 (1997): 270–71; H. George Fredrickson, *The Spirit of Public Administration* (San Francisco: Jossey-Bass, 1996); Montjoy and Watson, "A Case for Reinterpreted Dichotomy of Politics and Administration," 231–39.

5. Lyle J. Sumek, "Turbulent Times Require Courageous Leaders" (Presentation, Tennessee City Manager's Association Annual Conference, Gatlinburg, Tennessee, October 24, 2002).

6. James H. Svara, *Official Leadership in the City: Patterns of Conflict and Cooperation* (Oxford: Oxford University Press, 1990), 80.

7. James H. Svara, "U.S. City Managers and Administrators in a Global Perspective," in *The Municipal Yearbook*, 25–33 (Washington, D.C.: ICMA Press, 1999); and H. George Fredrickson, Brett Logan, and Curtis Wood, "Municipal Reform in Mayor-Council Cities: A Well-Kept Secret," *State and Local Government Review* 35, no. 1 (2003): 7–14.

8. Svara, *Official Leadership in the City.*

9. Deil S. Wright, "The City Manager as a Development Administrator," in *Comparative Urban Research*, ed. Robert T. Daland, 203–48 (Beverly Hills, Calif.: Sage, 1969).

10. Newell and Ammons, "Role Emphases of City Managers and Other Municipal Executives," 97–107.

11. Newell and Adams, "Role Emphases of City Managers."

12. Svara, *Official Leadership in the City.*

13. Robert L. Lineberry and Ira Sharkansky, *Urban Politics and Public Policy*, 3rd ed. (New York: Harper and Row, 1978), 164.

14. Svara, *Official Leadership in the City*, 104.

15. Douglas Yates, *The Ungovernable City* (Cambridge, Mass.: MIT Press, 1977).

16. Svara, *Official Leadership in the City*; Barbara Ferman, *Governing the Ungovernable City: Political Skill, Leadership and the Modern Mayor* (Philadelphia: Temple University Press, 1985); and Richard Feiock and James Clingermayer, "Municipal Representation, Executive Power, and Economic Development Policy Activity," *Policy Studies Journal* 15 (1986): 211–29.

17. Svara, *Official Leadership in the City*, 221.

18. Abney and Lauth, *The Politics of State and City Administration*, 195; and Alana Northrup and William H. Dutton, "Municipal Reform and Group Influence," *American Journal of Political Science* 22, no. 3 (1978): 691–711.

19. Thomas C. Beierle and Jerry Cayford, *Democracy in Practice. Public Participation in Environmental Decisions* (Washington, D.C.: Resources for the Future, 2002).

20. Abney and Lauth, *Politics of State and City Administration*, 195.

21. Michael J. Rich, Michael W. Giles, and Emily Stern, "Collaborating to Reduce Poverty: View From City Halls and Community-Based Organizations," *Urban Affairs Review* 37, no. 2 (2001): 184–204; Abney and Lauth, *Politics of State and City Administration*; and Camilla Stivers, "The Listening Bureaucrat: Responsiveness in Public Administration," *Public Administration Review* 54, no. 4 (1994): 364–69.

22. Michael D. Grimes et al., "Community Structure and Leadership Arrangements: A Multidimensional Analysis," *American Sociological Review* 69, no. 4 (1975): 1181–99.

23. Svara, *Official Leadership in the City*, 211.

4

Measuring and Comparing Municipal Service Quality

Wouldn't it be great if it were possible to identify all of the things that are within the ability of local officials to control that contribute to high levels of municipal service performance, particularly the policies, practices, and strategies that promote service quality, efficiency, and effectiveness? Beyond just identifying these things, how might the management and operation of municipal service regimes be different if it were possible to quantify and predict the specific impact that various policies, practices, and strategies have on service performance? For a given a level of taxation and fiscal resources, what levels of service quality, efficiency, and effectiveness are possible for cities to achieve? What would be the measurable value added to service performance achievements attributable to having a team of well-trained professional managers in charge of city services and programs?

Such speculations may remain scenes in a pleasant dream for public administrators for some time, but they help to remind us what might be possible if progress continues on measuring service performance and achievements. Robert Behn underscores the importance of continuing efforts to figure out how managers, legislators, and citizens can know whether government is doing a good job and delivering services and programs that produce desired results and maximum value for the taxes citizens pay to government.[1] Strategies to link planning, action, and evaluation within a performance management system are only among the more recent avenues of research.[2]

Since the 1960s, political scientists and public administration scholars have been trying to determine what impacts on local policies and services can be attributed to various features of municipal governments, particularly reformed structures.[3] Often, these studies produced mixed results and considerable debate about how to make valid and fair comparisons and how to measure service costs, efficiency, and performance. Only since the mid-1990s has the value of using truly comparable performance statistics in the context of a municipal benchmarking project received widespread recognition as both a valid and potentially useful approach to measuring performance and for learning what ideas and practices distinguish cities with high levels of service performance.[4] Comparative analysis is the approach shared by many previous and contemporary efforts to link service performance with policies and practices.

Yet there is one aspect of efforts to measure and compare municipal service performance that has received inadequate attention from public administration scholars but remains among the most salient concerns for public managers. This aspect is service quality. This chapter focuses on and explores the meaning of service quality, its two important dimensions, the factors that may affect citizens' perceptions of service quality, the points in the service process that might account for citizens' ratings of quality that are less than desired, and the indicators used to measure quality. We then use available indicators of service quality to distinguish three levels of service quality in four different services provided by the small communities in this study. Finally, we identify the factors that account for these differences in service quality and describe the value added to the level of service quality in those communities served by professional city managers. Our aim is to advance understanding of the meaning and measurement of service quality and to document any measurable differences in municipal service quality levels that are attributable to having professional city managers as chief executives.

THE CONCEPT OF SERVICE QUALITY

In a national survey of municipal managers in cities larger than 25,000, managers cited "difficulty in measuring the quality of municipal services and programs" as one of their most common problems in performance measurement.[5] The difficulty in measuring service quality may be one reason why less than 20 percent of all finance officers in small communities collect performance measures of local services.[6] Reaching an agreement on what service quality means may be a large part of the difficulty in measuring it.

Defining service quality is similar to trying to describe fine art: We recognize it when we experience it, but it is difficult to agree on a common metric for measuring it. Public administration scholars have recognized the importance of the quality of service dimension in making fair and accurate performance assessments for some time.[7] However, most of the theoretical and empirical research on service quality comes from scholars in marketing, advertising, or other fields connected with the nation's business schools.[8]

The preeminent theme in this research on service quality is that the opinion of the citizen or customer should figure prominently in any definition of the concept. Consequently, the closest thing to a consensus in the literature about the meaning of "service quality" is that it is whatever the customer or citizen says it is.

While a more precise definition of service quality with global application is problematic, what citizens think about public services is and should be paramount in a responsive, accountable democratic government.[9] Any conceptualization of the quality of a public service therefore must incorporate citizens' opinions. Marketing scholars have defined service quality as the character of a service that consistently meets or exceeds customers' needs and expectations.[10] From a public manager's perspective, service quality might be defined by criteria similar to how their performance often is judged: doing the right thing, well and fairly, first time, every time.

If citizens' views about the quality of a service are paramount, a challenge for local officials is to decide *which* citizens' opinions are relevant for determining the quality of a service. Depending on the service, there may be several groups in the community whose opinions matter but in different ways to local officials. For services provided to all citizens, everyone in the community could be considered a stakeholder since all receive some direct benefit. The opinions of stakeholders, or those who use or benefit from a service, certainly should figure prominently in evaluations of local service quality and service performance.

However, some programs or services benefit a more narrow constituency or clientele. Not everyone, for example, lives in public housing, uses city recreational facilities, needs emergency medical services, or visits the local library. What complicates matters is that although these services may be used by a subset of local residents, their funding may be dependent on a broader base of financial support. In deciding whose opinions should matter in service quality evaluations, local officials have to determine how to weigh the opinions of service users and nonuser taxpayers whose financial or political support may be important for sustaining those services.

Analyses of municipal service performance should seek to ascertain whether the city is "doing the right things" and also whether it is "doing things right." This suggests two levels of analysis: citywide and programmatic.[11] In the first, the opinions of all local taxpayers should be an important part of the calculus for deciding what services should be provided, their priority, and what level of service quality taxpayers are willing to support financially. It is important to reach a political consensus in the community about what citizens want, expect, or prefer in terms of the type and level of quality for various services and what level of service they are willing to support financially.

Otherwise, confusion may occur in actually trying to interpret citizen feed-back about service quality. For example, citizen opinion surveys typically attempt to measure how satisfied service users are with the quality of a partic-ular service. If 70 percent of the responses indicate at least some level of sat-isfaction while 30 percent indicate some level of dissatisfaction, how are managers supposed to use this information to improve services? What does this question really measure? Are some citizens indicating that they are dis-satisfied with the level of service provided, the actual performance of the serv-ice, or both? Survey data of this type have extremely limited decision utility.

The point is that some survey questions can measure what citizens think about the level and type of service provided, and some questions can measure what citizens think about the various aspects of the quality of a service per-formance experience.[12] The former relate to one dimension of service quality (is the community doing the right things?) and the latter relates to a different dimension (is the community doing things right?).

THE TWO DIMENSIONS OF SERVICE QUALITY

The labels we attach to these two dimensions are "input" and "output" service quality. Input service quality refers to the level of service designed or intended to be provided by a community. Communities vary in terms of the scope, nature, or character of a particular service, and each service may vary in its mode of delivery, frequency, intensity, coverage, or convenience.

For example, a community that provides daily police patrols of all residen-tial areas and crime-prone areas can be said to have a higher level of input quality for this service than a community that occasionally patrols only main business arteries. Similarly, some communities may provide twice-a-week backdoor collection of solid wastes while others collect waste weekly at the curb. Other communities may require residents to transport their waste to a central collection center. Likewise, fire protection may be provided at a high level of input service quality if a community chooses to invest in the facilities, infrastructure, and personnel that enable rapid deployment of firefighting resources in response to fire alarms anywhere within the corporate limits. On the other hand, a community that chooses to rely entirely on trained volun-teers or other on-call public employees to fight fires may be unable to respond to fire calls as quickly and could be considered to have a lower level of input service quality.

Our view is that measuring the level of input service quality provided by the community can facilitate fairer and more meaningful performance com-parisons. Unless differences in the level of service quality are accounted for, comparisons of outcomes on various performance measures, especially those that involve unit service costs, are inherently unfair and of little value for local officials interested in knowing how well they are doing their jobs.

The second aspect of the concept of service quality is output service quality. Output service quality refers to what citizens think about the performance of a service that they experience, especially whether that performance meets, exceeds, or falls short of their needs and expectations. While input service quality issues are best resolved by seeking a community-wide consensus about a desired level of service that citizens are willing to support financially, issues related to output service quality are best addressed as part of a program-level analysis of service performance. In other words, citizen feedback about what level of service they prefer is not helpful in making decisions about how to improve actual service performance and vice versa. The distinction between input and output quality reinforces the need to focus on the kind of citizen feedback local officials can use to reach decisions about the design of a service policy and improvement of a service performance, respectively.

CONCEPTUAL MODEL OF SERVICE QUALITY

There is much that we do know about how best to measure the output quality of a service, the extent to which certain contextual factors and circumstances in people's lives shape their perceptions of service quality, and how overall perceptions of service quality affect citizens' level of satisfaction with a service. To help advance understanding of the possible relationships among these factors, a conceptual model of service quality is presented that identifies sources for potential gaps between citizen needs, preferences, and expectations and their perceptions about the quality of a service performance.

This model suggests that the perceived quality of a service performance affects the level of citizen satisfaction with a service. In figure 4.1, the arrow between the perceived output quality of a service and citizen satisfaction with a service reflects the growing consensus about this causal direction.[13] Citizen perceptions of the quality of a service performance are antecedent to and shape their overall level of satisfaction with the service.

Output service quality and service satisfaction are considered to be distinct concepts. Perceptions of service quality are shaped by citizens' rating of a service performance based on the specific aspects of quality that they consider to be important for that service. Service quality perceptions are subjective assessments of actual service experiences. By contrast, service satisfaction judgments are influenced by a number of subjective cognitive and affective processes in addition to quality judgments. Such influences include emotions,

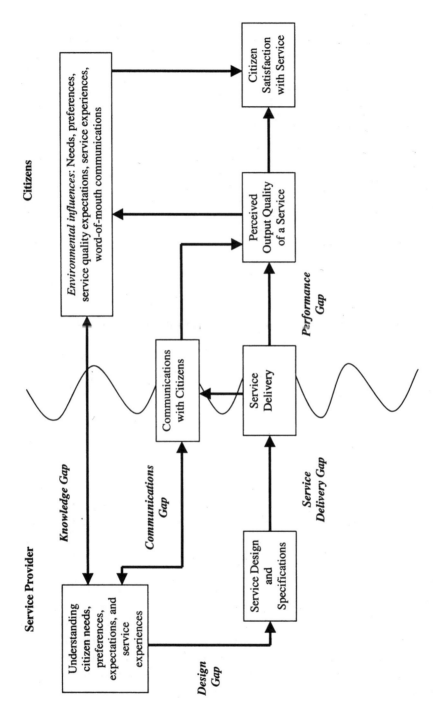

Citizens

Service Provider

Figure 4.1.   Conceptual Model of Service Quality and Potential Gaps That Affect Perceptions of Output Service Quality

word-of-mouth communications, or other events unrelated to a personal service experience or outside the control of a local service provider.[14] For instance, a citizen might believe that residents of another neighborhood receive a higher level of service for less taxes or that county residents receive a comparable service without paying city taxes. Such views may color how satisfied citizens are with the municipal service they receive.

Typical citizen surveys that measure overall service satisfaction have their public relations uses, but usually they only indicate what proportions of citizens are more or less satisfied with a service. They do not reveal *why* citizens hold the opinion they express or what aspects of a service meet or fall short of their needs or expectations. General measures of overall service satisfaction are not very useful indicators of service performance. For this reason, managers are rightfully skeptical about the utility of this information especially when survey results do not correspond to what they think actually occurs during service performance.

Our conceptual model assumes that citizens can provide fairly reliable evaluations of the quality of a service performance if they have some direct experience with or knowledge about the service and if the measures of these perceptions are crafted to tap the aspects of quality that citizens consider important for a particular service.[15] Further, it is based on the logic of "gap theory," which suggests there are multiple points in a service process at which a gap or difference may occur that could account for why citizens' perceptions of service quality do not meet or exceed their needs, preferences, or expectations.[16] Gap theory also is the logical underpinning for the SERVQUAL framework, which has been the subject of a growing volume of research in the field of marketing.[17]

Some scholars also have suggested that this framework has applicability to the public sector.[18] For this reason, it is useful to highlight the key respects in which the SERVQUAL model differs from our model. In SERVQUAL consumer perceptions of service quality are considered to be a function of whether a service performance matches the individual's *normative* performance expectations for that service. If a service meets or exceeds these expectations, the service is considered to be high quality. The SERVQUAL framework assumes that most consumers have the knowledge or information necessary to have an informed opinion about what constitutes an ideal, excellent quality service and that they use this metric to discern differences between what service they expect and what service they receive.

This assumption may apply to the private sector where purchases are the result of individual choices, but it is less likely to hold when considering the public service environment, in which most services are financed by compulsory taxes. Moreover, there are genuine differences among citizens' experience, information, knowledge, and interest in forming opinions about an ideal public service. Therefore, we think it is inappropriate to define the quality of a public service *exclusively* as the difference (or gap) between a normative performance expectation and a service performance experience. The risk of producing skewed results is especially high if some citizens have unreasonable or unrealistic service expectations. For example, a crime victim might expect a high-quality police performance to produce an immediate arrest of a perpetrator or a resident might expect same-day repair of a pothole reported on a residential cul-de-sac. Citizens may have a much easier time conceptualizing a realistic (and analytically useful) expectation for the performance of an appliance or a banking service than for a law enforcement, street repair, or other public service.

Our model assumes that residents' perceptions of the quality of a service performance are determined largely by their *actual* experience with the service. This perspective corresponds to the growing empirical evidence that casts doubt on the importance of a mental calculus involving an "ideal" versus an actual service experience. In other words, the perceived quality of a service performance is affected most by an actual service experience rather a perceived difference between an ideal and actual experience.

Within the two domains of "service provider" and "citizens," the model suggests five possible gaps or points in the process of providing a service that may account for the reasons why citizen perceptions of service performance quality are less than satisfactory or why citizen service ratings are lower than a performance target set by municipal officials.[19] In the service process, these gaps may occur at one or more stages, including performance, delivery, design, communications, and knowledge. The utility of this model as a diagnostic tool lies in the extent to which local officials review and analyze each point as a potential source for or cause of a perceived output quality service problem.

The Service Performance Gap

If citizens' level of satisfaction with a particular service is less than desired, many local officials understandably are inclined to focus first and sometimes exclusively on possible problems with the actual performance of a service. However, without feedback from recipients about *why* satisfaction levels may be less than desired, managers have little guidance about how to change service performance to improve satisfaction levels. The model indicates that a service performance gap may exist when citizens' experiences with a service do not meet their needs, preferences, or expectations on the aspects of quality that they consider to be important for that service. Once local officials have a baseline of what citizens think about the quality of services provided, quality of service performance targets can be established for services.

The threefold challenge is to identify the aspects or characteristics of service quality that are relevant to each service or program, determine their relative importance to the citizens who receive the service, and then measure how well citizens think the service was performed on each of those dimensions. Such information is analogous to an "intermediate outcome" for a service or program.[20] Measuring citizen opinions on service quality captures information distinct from efficiency and effectiveness. Measures of service quality should indicate which aspects of a service meet, exceed, or fall short of citizen needs and expectations. Analysis of the results can provide supervisors with useful guidance about what things may need to be improved to alter citizens' perceptions of service quality in the desired direction.

For example, the SERVQUAL model suggests that five aspects of service quality may be important to consumers: reliability, responsiveness, tangibles, assurance, and empathy.[21] Although some scholars have suggested that the SERVQUAL survey instrument has applicability for public services, we suggest particular aspects of output service quality that are considered to correspond with the nature of public services.[22]

Local officials should consider the applicability of at least four aspects of output service quality, devise survey questions that ascertain how important each quality aspect is to the service recipient, and then measure what citizens think about service performance on each aspect. The four aspects are reliability, employee interactions, physical aspects of the service, and service policies. Table 4.1 illustrates how these aspects of output service quality could be used to guide the design of survey questions that measure the performance of solid waste collection and a building permit services office.[23]

The *reliability* of a service refers to the extent that a service provides what was promised, when it was promised. Timeliness, dependability, and consistency are among the most important elements of reliability. Doing the right things well or accurately first time, every time is a feature of a highly reliable service. Depending on the service, reliability may entail whether a promised level of service is provided at the same interval promptly and consistently or whether the same level, type, and accuracy of service is provided at all times by different staff or employees.

Employee interaction with citizens refers to an aspect of output quality that is especially important when public employees have contact with the public. Depending on the nature of the service, the kind of impression that employees make on the service recipient may be a result of several factors. These include

**Table 4.1. Potential Measures for the Aspects of Service Quality:
Solid Waste Collection and Building Permit Services**

Quality Dimension	Solid Waste Collection	Building Permit Office
Reliability	—A reliable or dependable waste collection service is one in which wastes are always collected on the day scheduled. How would you rate the reliability of the city's waste collection service during the last [time period]? (1 = not reliable at all; 5 = very reliable) —During the last [time period] was there ever an occasion when your household's wastes were NOT collected on the day scheduled? If yes, about how many times did this occur? —During the last [time period], did a waste collection crew ever cause damage to your waste bin? —In your neighborhood, please rate how careful waste collection crews are about not spilling any waste on the street when emptying bins. (1 = not very careful; 5 = very careful)	—How would you rate the performance of city staff with respect to the amount of time it took to process your building permit application? (1= very poor; 5 = very good) —Did city staff make any errors in reviewing any building permit applications you submitted in 2004? —For the building permit application(s) that you filed in 2004, about how long did you have to wait for someone to accept your application(s)? —Were you provided with information about how to appeal a decision by the building permit office?
Employee Interaction	—During the last [time period], did you have occasion to contact the city to report a waste collection problem or to make a request? If yes, please rate the helpfulness of the response that you received. (1= not helpful at all; 5 = very helpful)	—Overall, how would you rate the helpfulness, knowledge, courtesy, and accuracy of information provided by staff in the building permit office with whom you interacted?
Physical Aspects	—Does the size (or type) of waste bin provided meet the needs of your household?	—How would rate the accessibility of the permit office and ease of use and clarity of application forms?
Service Policies	—What kind of job does the city do in publicizing the schedule for curbside leaf collection in different neighborhoods during the fall season? (1= very poor; 5 = very good). —Currently everyone pays the same for waste disposal regardless of how much waste is thrown out. Would you favor or oppose a policy that would charge customers a fee based on the size of the waste bin that they request? (e.g., a smaller bin (25 gal.) would cost less than a larger bin (55 gal).)	—Did you visit the city's website to obtain information about the zoning ordinance provisions for the site(s) on which you propose to build? If yes, please rate on the following scale how easy or difficult it was to obtain the information you wanted. (1 = very difficult; 5 = very easy). —Please rate the overall level of convenience of the building permit application process.

the employees' receptivity to an individual's needs or problems and what citizens think about their knowledge, helpfulness, courtesy, friendliness, trustworthiness, attitude, and willingness to listen. Also relevant are what citizens think about employees' competence to perform a service accurately and carefully, their communication skills, their problem-solving ability, and their ability to use available technology.

The *physical aspects of a service* can include the condition, appearance, safety, adequacy, and capacity of the facilities, equipment, materials, or personnel connected with a service or the environment in which the service is provided. For example, citizens' perceptions of the quality of drop-off recycling collection service can be measured by asking users about the accessibility, ease of use, cleanliness, clarity of signage, and helpfulness of any on-site staff. Likewise, the location, cleanliness, perceived safety, and choices offered in a park or recreation facility may affect how users perceive the quality of that service. For any service that involves an interaction between the citizen and a public facility or space, the physical aspects of that experience will shape public perceptions of service quality.

Service policies that govern the provision of a service also affect citizen perceptions of service quality. The policies a community adopts for providing a service have implications for the perceived convenience, accessibility, flexibility, adequacy, availability, and value of a service. Service policies determine hours of operation, expectations for citizens in the coproduction of a service, methods for handling citizen complaints or service requests, and the availability of alternatives for conducting municipal business.

Policies that broaden citizen choices are likely to be perceived as enhancing the convenience of a service. For example, if citizens have the option of applying for permits, paying bills, or obtaining service information online at the municipal website, the perceived convenience of a service likely will be higher. A community that permits citizens to appeal parking tickets online may experience fewer complaints about the time it takes to process such issues. Likewise, a policy to enhance collection of unpaid fines by withholding certain city services to scofflaws may enhance perceptions of service equity. On the other hand, the use of photo-cams at intersections to identify vehicles that speed through red lights may be convenient for local law enforcement officials but engenders considerable animus among citizens. The important point is that service policies can have a significant impact on the extent to which citizens perceive a service to be convenient, accessible, efficient, and equitable. These perceptions can shape opinions about whether government is "customer-driven," mired in red tape, or concerned chiefly about ways to lighten citizens' pocketbooks.

The Service Delivery Gap

The genesis for a problem with service quality may originate in a stage of the service process other than in the actual performance of the service. A gap in service delivery occurs when a disparity arises between the level of service quality intended to be provided and the level of service quality actually delivered. A specified level of service promised in communications with citizens may not be realized in practice. Employees may be unable, for a variety of reasons, to deliver the kind of service designed to be provided. The service provided may be performed well, but employees may be unable to sustain the level, frequency, or intensity of service intended or promised by the city.

Several factors may account for a service delivery gap. The most typical causes are rooted in problems related to the adequacy or capacity of available resources for a service that may prevent or frustrate employee efforts to provide the service at a promised or expected level. Resource problems may occur because of equipment breakdowns, inadequate facilities, or poor supervision. Some causes may be entirely outside local control. Devastating natural disasters or acts of terrorism obviously hamper the ability to provide an expected level of service.

The Knowledge, Service Design, and Communication Gaps

Three other interrelated points in the service delivery process may affect citizens' perceptions of output service quality and their consequent satisfaction with the quality of a municipal service. Each of these three potential problem areas relates to input service quality issues but may affect perceptions of output service quality. A knowledge gap occurs when local officials lack complete knowledge about or clear understanding of what citizens need, expect, prefer, or will support with respect to the type, array, level, or cost of services in the community. In other words, there may be a disparity between a level of input service quality that citizens expect or want and what city officials think that citizens prefer or want. This knowledge gap almost inevitably leads to a service design gap in which local service priorities, resource allocations, and service specifications do not correspond very well with the kind and level of input service quality services that citizens need or want and are willing to support financially.

The genesis for both the knowledge and design gaps is a communication gap. Local officials may not have a firm understanding of what level of services citizens prefer or are willing to support financially, and citizens may not have information about what outcomes are produced or achieved by the services provided by the locality. The typical result of this communication gap is an ongoing, aggravated struggle between local government's efforts to provide services at some level deemed to be adequate by local officials and citizens who gripe about high local taxes for services and programs whose accomplishments and value are unclear or unknown.

While some segment of the public may remain inattentive or unconcerned about local government performance, regardless of how well services may be performed for a particular level of resource support, it is important for public managers to engage in quality measurement and "managerial thinking" as part of a continuing effort to improve service outcomes.[24] Measuring what citizens think about the various dimensions of service quality can help operating officials make decisions about how best to improve a service in ways that will have the most significant positive impact on citizen perceptions of service quality. As part of a performance measurement system, this information along with measures of efficiency and service outcomes should figure prominently in reports to and communications with citizens and council members about the value of local services and what impacts and accomplishments have been attained by current levels of financial support. This may be one of the few strategies local officials have for educating citizens about what they receive for their local tax dollars. All too often, when such information is available it rarely escapes beyond the walls of city hall.

In the future, it may be possible for local officials to compare their locality's service performance with that of other cities offering a comparable level of input service quality. When communities move beyond collection of just raw workload and output data for reporting and accountability purposes and use higher order measures of service quality, efficiency, and effectiveness, managers will have the type of information that can help them to attain service objectives. Line managers need performance information that they can use to make more informed operating decisions about resource deployment, scheduling, service routes, equipment, and personnel needs. Performance achievements then need to be shared with and marketed to both local elected leaders and service constituencies.

Ideally, the information from a local government performance measurement system should enable managers to describe and communicate the quality characteristics, effectiveness, and impacts of local services and programs. They should also be able to estimate what specific additional benefits would accrue to citizens and what progress could be made in addressing particular problems or needs if additional resources could be allocated to that service or program. Of course, the reality of local government performance measurement practices has not yet attained this ideal. However, with continued incremental progress in the actual use of performance measures, the opportunities will increase to make a public case for the value of existing services and the benefits of investing additional resources in these services.

By emphasizing the importance of citizen opinions in service quality ratings and by sharing what value and results are obtained from local services, more local residents may consider themselves to be stakeholders in an array of services and programs that extend beyond those they use or benefit from directly. Enhanced communication between local government and residents can only help to broaden understanding of, if not appreciation for, what government does and how well it does it.

THE VALUE OF MEASURING INPUT SERVICE QUALITY

As noted, our view is that performance comparisons among communities with dissimilar levels of input quality are inherently unfair and may actually impede efforts to disseminate information about "better" policies, practices, and strategies that can be adapted by communities with vastly different resources.[25] Comparing service performance among cities with comparable levels of input service quality may enhance the perceived fairness and utility of these efforts. Local officials may be more willing to adapt the things that similar cities claim are helpful in improving service performance.

It is logical to expect a linkage between the input and output service quality. Absent an ability or political consensus to increase the level of service inputs, the issue is whether a smaller community with limited fiscal resources, peculiar service needs, and different policy priorities can readily adapt many of the best practices employed by cities that offer a higher level of service quality and that differ on other key environmental features. Would the inability to afford a higher level of input service quality necessarily mean, for example, that a community could not hope to improve response time performances in fire protection? We think local officials are more likely to consider performance comparisons among cities with similar levels of input service quality to be fairer and of greater value for potential adaptation of the best practices. A further refinement of performance comparisons among cities that provide the same level of input service quality is to match cities with comparable workloads and service demands. Proximate measures of these factors, for example, might be population and geographic size.

Within the context of benchmarking efforts in particular, this approach to comparative performance analysis can help to move the practice of performance measurement beyond mere data collection and reporting to the actual use of this information for making decisions about resource allocation and service improvement. Accordingly, public administration scholars and practitioners should revisit their analyses of urban services to devise criteria that can help to distinguish different levels of input service quality. These classifications can help localities identify suitable partners for performance comparison and benchmarking efforts. The objective is to facilitate identification of cities with similar service operations and to increase the prospects for adoption of service improvement ideas gained from the higher performers.

Efforts to distinguish different levels of municipal input service quality are in their nascency. One framework for classifying the input quality levels of solid waste recycling services, for instance, suggests that differences in policies affecting the convenience of recycling can be used to identify quality of service classes among communities.[26] Absent a consensus about how best to accomplish this for a broad range of services provided by municipalities, this study focuses on a narrower range of commonly provided services for which a limited number of indicators of service quality have been collected. These services include fire protection, police protection, building code enforcement, and solid waste recycling.

Predicate to applying indicators of input service quality for these services, it is useful to identify the scope of functional responsibilities among the small communities in this study. The distribution of the functional responsibilities performed by cities has been the subject of considerable research and has been shown to be related to revenue, expenditure, and debt patterns as well as the responsiveness of local governments.[27] However, the U.S. Census of Governments only collects these data for cities larger than 25,000. Consequently, the data collected from our national survey on the functional responsibilities of small cities represents the only known measurement of such a distribution.

Table 4.2 indicates that more than 90 percent of all small communities provide six of the ten listed services. These services include police and fire protection, street maintenance, parks and recreation, water and sewer utility services, and solid waste collection and disposal. More than 83 percent engage

Table 4.2.   Distribution of Services Provided by Small Cities

Service	N responses	N provide	Percent
Police protection	508	503	99.0
Fire protection	504	494	98.0
Street maintenance	508	495	97.4
Parks and recreation	427	422	94.8
Water and sewer service	498	470	94.4
Solid waste collection and disposal	502	452	90.0
Economic/community development	508	426	83.8
Public housing	493	350	70.0
Public transportation	496	276	55.6
Education	418	84	20.0

in an economic and community development function, while only 20 percent of small cities contribute financially to a local public school system. Since most small cities provide some type of service in the four functions selected for analysis of input service quality, indicators of service quality are identified for these commonly provided services.

INDICATORS OF INPUT SERVICE QUALITY

Ideally, the kind of information most helpful in distinguishing different levels of service among cities are data for service budgets, staff qualifications, staff levels and experience, available equipment and technology, type of facilities, and practices and policies used by service departments. Some of this information might be obtained through mail or telephone surveys. A combination of personal interviews and site visits would probably yield a richer understanding of these service characteristics. It is conceivable that staff connected with a university or state municipal technical assistance programs could collect such information from communities for analyses of input service quality.

For the small communities included in this study, resource constraints dictated that we use proximate measures of input service quality with at least some potential to distinguish the different levels of service among fire protection, police protection, building code enforcement, and solid waste management services. The objective is to illustrate the merit of distinguishing levels of input quality for different services and to understand the community and governmental features that characterize small communities with different levels of input service quality.

Police Services

In this era of "community policing," small municipal police departments may be expected to perform a variety of services including law enforcement, crime prevention, traffic control, protection of civil rights and liberties, solving crimes, and preventing terrorism. The Commission on Accreditation for Law Enforcement Agencies, Inc. (CALEA) has devised standards for law enforcement agencies and administers an accreditation process through which law enforcement agencies may demonstrate voluntarily that they meet professionally recognized criteria for excellence in management and service delivery.[28] However, an examination of the CALEA list of accredited members indicated that police departments from larger cities are predominant.[29] Only about 3 percent (fifteen cities) of the small communities in our study have attained CALEA accreditation.

Absent detailed programmatic information on small city police departments, the proximate measure used to distinguish different levels of law
enforcement service provided by small communities is the ratio of full-time
sworn police officers (excluding civilians) per one thousand population.[30]
This ratio is a proximate indicator of what a community has chosen to invest
in the human resources for community law enforcement and protection. The
mean ratio for all of the cities in this study is 2.095 sworn officers per one
thousand population. However, since city size is inversely related to this ratio,
we account for differences in workload that affect the staffing levels required
or needed in a community.

To help account for differences in workload, cities were divided into three
groups based on population size: less than 5,000 population, 5,000 to 14,999,
and 15,000 or more. Each of these population groups was divided further into
two groups based on whether the city's population density (people per square
mile) was above or below the mean for that population group. This procedure
yielded six groups of cities (two in each population class), the members of
which were generally similar in terms of population size and density.

Then, for each of the six groups of cities, three levels of service were identified. The communities with sworn officer ratios in the highest 25 percent for
each group were assigned a service level of "1." Cities with ratios either 15
percent above or below the group mean were assigned a "2," and the remaining cities were assigned a value of "3." The result consists of six groups of
cities with three levels of service identified for each group. This method captures a difference in the level of community investment in police while
accounting for differences in population size and density that may affect
staffing levels.

Table 4.3 shows the distribution of 406 cities for which data are available
on the number of sworn officers, population size, and population density.
Approximately 29 percent of small cities were classified in category 1, indicating that they provide a "high" sworn officer ratio. About 31 percent of
cities had a category 2 or mid-level ratio. The remaining 40 percent of cities
in category 3 or basic level had sworn officer ratios no higher than 15 percent
below the mean for their respective group. One indicator of the face validity
of this proximate measure of input service quality for police is that each of the
communities assigned a value of "1," which connotes a high service level,
also had achieved CALEA accreditation.

While a linkage may exist between the level of input and output service
quality, the distinctions in input quality among municipal police services do
not measure anything about the actual performance of local police departments. In other words, some cities classified as providing a basic level of input
service quality may perform their functions as efficiently or effectively as

Table 4.3. Police Staffing Levels, Sworn Officers per 1,000 Population

| | Cities Less Than 5,000 | | | | | | Cities 5,000 to 14,999 | | | | | | Cities 15,000 to 25,000 | | | | | |
| | Density below mean | | | Density above mean | | | Density below mean | | | Density above mean | | | Density below mean | | | Density above mean | | |
Service Level	Ratio range	N	%	Ratio range	N	%	Ratio range	N	%	Ratio range	N	%	Ratio range	N	%	Ratio range	N	%
High (1) N = 117	4.59–2.68	20	29.0	4.28–2.44	11	26.2	5.05–2.44	32	26.2	4.16–2.31	22	31.0	5.00–2.47	22	32.4	3.10–2.17	10	29.4
Mid (2) N = 127	2.61–2.13	16	23.2	2.42–1.78	16	38.1	2.38–1.97	28	23.0	2.30–1.63	24	33.8	2.44–1.73	31	45.6	2.11–1.47	12	35.3
Basic (3) N = 162	2.12–1.28	33	47.8	1.76–1.07	15	35.7	1.96–.97	62	50.8	1.58–.90	25	35.2	1.71–.37	15	22.1	1.35–1.01	12	35.3
Totals		69	100		42	100		122	100		71	100		68	100		34	100

other cities that provide a higher level of input service quality. That determination is beyond the scope of this study.

What is the value of this input quality classification scheme? It groups cities into comparable levels of input service quality so that later performance analysis will not be confounded by differences in the level of service provided. The implicit assumption is that high performers may exist in each service quality class and that some of these might have service operations, strategies, or policies worthy of adaptation or emulation by other communities in the same class whose service performance is not quite as high.

Grouping cities in service quality classes may facilitate identification of more suitable partners for a service benchmarking effort. For local officials, it addresses the comparability component in the common question about what "similar" cities are doing differently to achieve a higher level of service performance. By holding input service quality "constant," service performance comparisons are fairer and potentially more useful since the prospects for adaptation of practices may be greater among cities with comparable levels of input service quality.

Fire Protection Services

The Insurance Services Office (ISO) is an independent organization that serves the property/casualty insurance industry by collecting information on the quality of public fire protection in 45,000 fire districts in forty-six states. These data are used to help establish appropriate fire insurance premiums for residential and commercial properties.[31] Evaluations of municipal fire protection efforts in Idaho, Louisiana, Mississippi, and Washington are provided by rating bureaus in those states using guidelines generally similar to those established by the ISO. The ISO's Public Protection Classification (PPC) program collects data on fire protection services using a Fire Suppression Rating Schedule (FSRS). The ISO assigns a public protection classification that ranges from 1 to 10, with a class 1 representing the highest level of protection and a class 10 indicating that a fire department has no public water supply or does not meet the minimum standards for fire protection established by the National Fire Protection Association (NFPA).

Communities that have better PPC classifications experience lower fire losses than communities with poorer classifications. The ISO finds that the cost of fire losses for homeowners' policies in communities graded in Class 9 is 65 percent higher than in communities graded Class 5.[32] Accordingly, a community's ISO classification affects the insurance premiums paid by local homeowners and businesses. While the actual dollar value varies by state, the price of fire insurance in communities with a higher level of protection generally is substantially less than in communities with a lower level of protection.

The components of the PPC classifications include features of the fire department's equipment inventory, staffing levels, fire station distribution, and maintenance and testing practices (50 percent); community water supply features such as fire hydrant availability, distribution and condition, and the adequacy of water pressure and supplies (40 percent); fire alarm practices that include assessments of the adequacy of communications systems, staffing, and dispatching; and how well the fire department receives and dispatches fire alarms (10 percent).[33]

The use of ISO classifications to measure municipal fire department performance is clearly inappropriate.[34] However, since the PPC classifications primarily measure inputs for community fire service, these ratings represent a reasonable method for comparing the different levels of the input quality of fire protection among cities. Ammons observed that in smaller cities, "volunteer firefighters still play a major role" with all volunteer or mostly volunteer firefighters comprising the vast majority of small town fire departments.[35] However, the reliance on volunteers in small town fire departments does not necessarily mean that the residents of those communities have an inadequate level of fire protection service.

Table 4.4 compares the municipal PPC ratings for all cities rated by ISO in 2000 with the 1999 ratings attained by the small cities that are included in this study.[36] The profile of PPC ratings for small cities indicates that nearly 80 percent attained a very respectable Class 4, 5, or 6 level. Compared to the

Table 4.4. National and Small City Distributions of Public Protection Classifications for Fire Protection Services

ISO Classification	All Cities		Small Cities	
	N	percent	N	percent
Class 1	42	.09	0	0
Class 2	310	.68	8	1.6
Class 3	1,182	2.59	46	9.2
Class 4	3,147	6.91	129	25.7
Class 5	5,653	12.42	161	32.1
Class 6	7,436	16.34	111	22.1
Class 7	6,818	14.98	15	3.0
Class 8	3,875	8.52	3	.6
Class 9	15,627	34.34	29	5.8
Class 10	1,414	3.12	0	0
Totals	45,504	100	502	100

Note: Where a fire district has more than one PPC rating, the better rating was selected.

national averages, there are proportionally more small city fire departments that achieved Class 2 through Class 5 ratings.

For purposes of comparing the input quality of fire services among small cities, the 54 communities with Class 2 or 3 ratings are categorized as providing a "high" level of input service quality; the 401 cities with Class 4, 5, or 6 ratings are categorized as providing a "mid"-level of input service quality; and the remaining 47 cities with lower ratings are classified as providing a "basic" level of input service quality. An analysis of these input quality groups and city size indicates that localities with more than 15,000 residents were somewhat more likely to have a "high" level of input quality than less populous cities (24 percent versus 12 percent). However, large majorities of cities in each population group (less than 5,000, 5,000 to 14,999, and 15,000 or more) were included in the "mid-level" input quality class.

Building Code Enforcement Services

Some type of building code enforcement was provided by about 83 percent of small communities. The Insurance Services Office provides the only known comparative assessment of community efforts to adopt and enforce building codes. Their evaluation instrument, called the Building Code Effectiveness Grading Schedule (BCEGS), is used to assess the building code adopted by a community and to measure how well the city enforces the code, with special emphasis on mitigation of losses from natural hazards. The ISO staff collect relevant community information from questionnaires and from on-site inspections.

The BCEGS evaluations may cover residential and commercial properties or just one type of property. Participating communities receive a grade that may range from 1 to 10, with a 1 representing exemplary commitment to building code enforcement and a 10 signifying a level of protection less than the desired minimum. The ISO assigns rating credits that apply to particular ranges of BCEGS classifications, specifically cities in the 1 to 3, 4 to 7, 8 to 9, or 10 classes.[37] Higher BCEGS ratings mean that a city has adopted adequate codes and does a better job of enforcing them. A Class 10 rating means that the community is not eligible for a BCEGS discount. As a product sold to insurance companies, these ratings help insurers to establish a rational linkage between risk and rates. Cities with higher ratings are expected to demonstrate a better loss experience and a lower risk of catastrophic-related damage. Local insurance rates typically reflect that lower risk level. BCEGS ratings are used only as credits. This means that local insurance rates do not increase just because a community may receive a lower rating. Rather, some residents who live in cities that experience a rating increase may benefit by receiving a discount or credit on their insurance costs.

**Table 4.5. National and Small City Building Code Enforcement
Grades for Commercial Structures**

BCEGS Classifications	All Cities		Small Cities	
	N	*percent*	*N*	*percent*
Class 1	4	.04	0	0
Class 2	137	1.6	3	.7
Class 3	1,143	13.4	38	9.0
Class 4	2,461	29.9	90	21.4
Class 5	2,193	25.8	85	20.2
Class 6	914	10.7	61	14.5
Class 7	905	10.6	29	6.9
Class 8	481	5.6	23	5.5
Class 9	199	2.3	21	5.0
Class 10	53	.62	6	1.4
98 or 99	n.a.	n.a.	65	15.4
Totals	8490	100	421	100

n.a. = not available.

The main incentives that city officials have for improving their rating is the prospect of reducing insurance rates on buildings constructed after a rating is elevated and the reduction of injuries and loss of life in the wake of a catastrophic event. The primary difference between the ISO's fire classification system and the BCEGS ratings is that changes to a community's fire classification affect potential risk to all structures, while a change in building inspection service only affects the potential risk to structures built after a change in classification.

The ISO regularly evaluates community building code enforcement efforts in about 8,500 communities in forty-five states about every five years, or more frequently if the community requests it.[38] Cities in Idaho, Kansas, Louisiana, Mississippi, and Washington do not participate in the ISO BCEGS ratings. All of these states except Kansas choose to have state rating bureaus evaluate municipal building code enforcement.

Table 4.5 compares BCEGS ratings for all participating U.S. cities and for the small communities in this study. These proportions indicate that small cities generally have lower (better) BCEGS ratings than other cities in the ISO rating population. The differences are especially large for Classes 2 through 5. Conversely, small cities are more than twice as likely to have a Class 9 or 10 rating compared to other cities that participate in the BCEGS rating program.

Inspection of the items evaluated in the BCEGS questionnaire suggests that this rating system is useful for distinguishing the level of effort communities make in building inspections as measured against accepted industry standards. Following the credit ranges established by the ISO, small cities are grouped into three levels of service. The 41 cities in BCEGS Classes 2 or 3 are categorized as providing a "high" level of input service quality. The 265 cities in Classes 4 through 7 are categorized as providing a "mid"-level of input service quality, and the 44 cities in Classes 8 and 9 are classified as providing a "basic" level of input service quality. There are 71 small cities that have ratings that make them ineligible for BCEGS discounts (coded 10, 99, or 98). These communities are considered to provide an inadequate level of building code enforcement for purposes of comparing input service quality.

Solid Waste Recycling Services

As an aspect of solid waste management, recycling has become a popular way for citizens to support environmental conservation and to help extend the life of local landfills. By 1998 more than 9,000 curbside programs and 12,000 recyclable drop-off centers had sprouted up across the nation. Increasing levels of citizen participation in this coproduced service helped to boost the national recycling rate from 9 percent in 1989 to 28 percent in 1999.[39] While 90 percent of the small cities in this study provide solid waste collection and disposal services, only about two-thirds have some type of solid waste recycling program. In about 13 percent of these cities, recycling service is contracted out to private or nonprofit organizations, while in about 2 percent the county operates the recycling program within the municipality.

To compare the level of recycling service provided by small cities in 1999, recycling programs were classified based on their relative convenience for citizens.[40] The most convenient recycling programs were considered to be those that provide both curbside and drop-off recycling options for citizens. Cities with both types of opportunities for recycling participation were classified as providing a "high" level of service. The communities that provided only curbside recycling were classified as offering a "mid"-level service. Finally, the cities that provided a "basic" level of service required citizens who wished to recycle to take their recyclable materials to a materials collection station.

Table 4.6 shows the distribution of recycling program types and service levels in all U.S. cities and in small communities. Compared to the distribution of all U.S. cities that offered recycling, fewer small cities offered both curbside and drop-off recycling. Proportionally, about twice as many small cities offered only drop-off recycling compared to the national average. However, the largest proportion of small cities still provided curbside recycling for at least some materials.

Table 4.6.   U.S. and Small Town Recycling Programs by Type and Level of Service

Program Type and Service Level	All U.S. Cities*		Small Cities	
	N	Percent	N	Percent
Curbside and drop-off (high level)	415	62.1	69	21.0
Curbside only (mid-level)	137	20.5	147	44.7
Drop-off only (basic level)	116	17.4	113	34.3
Totals	668	100	329	100
No recycling service	n.a.	n.a.	173	34.4

*Based on national survey results in David H. Folz, "Service Quality and Benchmarking the Performance of Municipal Services," *Public Administration Review* 64, no. 2 (2004): 209–20.
n.a. = not available or not applicable.

INPUT SERVICE QUALITY LEVELS AMONG SMALL COMMUNITIES

The method used to classify cities into one of three overall input quality levels was driven by two objectives: to preserve the largest number of cases across four services and to capture the most important distinctions between the different levels of input service quality offered by small cities. The city scores on the four services provided the basis for the overall classification of input service quality. For a city to be included in the analysis, input quality scores had to exist for at least three of the four services. Considering the importance of and larger budgets for police and fire, these two services received greater weight in the classification of overall input quality.

Police and fire scores were used as initial qualifying screens for a quality classification. For a city to be considered for the high-level service category, the combined score for both police and fire had to be 3 or lower. If a score existed only for police or fire, that score had to be a "1" for the city to be considered for the high-level service category. For cities that qualified for possible inclusion in the high-level category after these screens, the score for building inspections and recycling services had to be either a "1" or a "2." If values for both services existed, the combined sum had to equal 3 or less.

For cities to be considered in the mid-quality service category, the combined score for both police and fire values had to equal 4. If a score was available for only police or fire, that score had to be a "2." For the cities that qualified for possible inclusion in the mid-level service category, the scores for building inspections and recycling services had to be either a "1" or a "2." The sum of both of these values could not exceed 4.

After application of these screens, the remaining cities were classified in the basic service category. These cities had a combined score for police and fire services of 5 or more. For cities with a value for only one of these services that value was a "3." The combined scores for building inspection and recycling for cities in the basic service category were either 5 or 6. As expected, each of the individual service scores had a high level of correlation at a statistically significant level with the overall measure of input service quality.

This method yielded an overall input service quality score for 436 cities or more than 85 percent of the cities in this study. The distribution of small cities in each classification of overall input service quality is high (1)—81 cities, 18.6 percent; mid (2)—202 cities, 46.4 percent; and basic (3)—153 cities, 34.9 percent.

This distribution indicates that the residents of almost two-thirds (65 percent) of small cities enjoyed an overall level of input service quality that exceeded what this analysis defined as basic. The scores for overall input service quality indicate that most of America's small cities have invested in a service infrastructure for the functions examined that exceeds what we define as basic. There is inherently nothing wrong or inadequate with offering a basic level of service. The interesting finding in this analysis is that the majority of small communities provided a level of service that exceeded this basic level.

This finding suggests that just because a community is small in size, its level of service quality is not necessarily lower than that provided by larger cities. The employees of small cities may be just as experienced, knowledgeable, and proficient, and the service infrastructure of small towns may be just as extensive, sophisticated, and appropriate for the environments in which they operate as that in some larger jurisdictions.

Building on this illustration, a more extensive and specific set of service quality indicators could be employed to classify levels of quality for different services. Service performance among cities with similar service levels could then be compared. This approach may enhance the prospects for adapting whatever methods, processes, practices, or policies are linked to high performance among cities with the same service quality level.

EXPLAINING THE DIFFERENCES IN INPUT SERVICE QUALITY

The measure of overall input service quality is a cross-sectional indicator of the level, scope, or extent of service that small communities have decided to invest in particular local government functions. Community features that logically may be related to a community's level of input quality include population size, wealth, local educational attainment, and metropolitan status. Do citizens and government officials in larger, wealthier, more highly educated, and metro- or micropolitan cities expect or provide a higher level of input quality? In addition, political factors such as type of governmental structure and type of chief executive may help to explain differences in community input service quality.

Table 4.7 shows the distribution of small communities with different levels of input service quality among the categories of population size, metropolitan status, and median household income. Analysis of the bivariate relationships between these variables and overall service quality scores indicates that city size, metropolitan status, and median household income are related to service quality level.[41] The cities that provide a higher level of input service quality tend to be larger, be located in micropolitan or metropolitan statistical areas, and have a higher median household income.

The relationships between input service quality and political variables are shown in table 4.8. Both political features of small communities also are related to the level of service quality at a statistically significant level.[42] These results indicate that communities with city managers are more likely to have a higher level of input service quality. Likewise, cities with adaptive and administrative political structures are more likely to have a higher level of input service quality than cities with a political structure. These findings suggest that having a city manager as chief executive had consequences in terms of service quality level. In addition to their more extensive involvement in the various dimensions of the governmental process and their distinct pattern of consultative decision making, city managers appear to have a role in promoting higher levels of input service quality in their communities.

Accurate attribution is an issue of primary concern that attends any suggestion that professional managers promote higher levels of input service quality. In other words, to what extent are more populous and wealthier cities also more likely to have city managers or adaptive and political government structures? Do local political structures really matter or is it just a question of community size, wealth, or education? To ascertain whether the type of local chief executive or government structure has any independent effects on the overall measure of input service quality, the relationships between the political variables and service quality were examined within the categories of community variables such as population size and wealth, in effect controlling for or holding constant the effects of these variables.[43]

Bivariate analyses indicated that larger cities were more likely to have city managers as their chief executive. However, no relationships existed between a city's median household income or educational attainment and its type of chief executive. Larger cities also were more likely to have an administrative type of government structure. Smaller cities are more likely to have either an adapted or political structure. Cities with higher median incomes are more likely to have an administrative type of government structure. However, no relationship existed between educational attainment and type of government structure.

of input service quality. No significant relationship remained between service quality level and government structure for cities with lower median household incomes.[47]

These controls for the effects of population size and city wealth helped to specify the particular groups of cities for which the type of executive and government structure mattered in terms of input service quality. The connection between a high level of input service quality and having a city manager and administrative type of government structure was most pronounced for small cities with larger populations. The connection between these variables for cities in the two small populations groups was in the same direction, but the magnitude of the relationships did not attain the threshold for statistical significance.

In terms of city wealth, the communities with median household incomes below the mean for all small cities and that had a city manager as their chief executive were much more likely to have a higher level of input service quality. For cities with median incomes above the group mean, having an administrative structure was linked to having a higher level of input service quality.

From a substantive perspective, these findings correspond to the conclusions reached by previous researchers who observed that professional city management and government structure have important local policy consequences.[48] This analysis provides some evidence for a statistically significant and substantively important connection between executive leadership by a professional city manager operating in an administrative form of government structure and the level of service quality provided.

In the early urban research on the impacts of governmental form on "service efficiency" (typically measured as per capita expenditures), there was an initial failure to account for differences in the functional scope of local governments. This was one reason for the divergent findings about the impacts of "reformed" government.[49] Failure to account for differences in the level of input service quality also may have accounted for some of the divergent findings about the impact of professionalism in managing urban services. Higher input service quality may cost more, and since the cities that provide a higher input service quality are more likely to have city managers as their chief executives, this confounding variable may have accounted for some findings that suggested little or no difference in service efficiency between reformed and unreformed government structures.

Why does a connection exist between type of executive, type of government structure, and the level of input service quality? The findings discussed in chapter 3 indicate that city managers exhibited a higher level of involvement in each of the dimensions of the governmental process, that they consulted more consistently with more service stakeholders, and that they were as responsive as elected mayors to the concerns of local interest groups. Building on these findings, we speculate that the professional values, training, and expertise of city and town managers and administrators must have something to do with promoting or encouraging advances in the level of urban services provided in their communities. City managers operating in administrative government structures may continue to hold an advantage over elected mayors who preside in political cities when it comes to facilitating collaborative civic authority and injecting expert administration into the delivery of urban services.[50]

While both mayors and city managers may be equally committed to promoting the public welfare and protecting the public's safety, our findings indicate that city managers may have more success in advancing these goals in their communities, at least to the extent that a higher level of urban services may offer enhanced prospects for realizing these goals. Consequently, one of the dividends for cities that have city managers and administrative structures is the development or maintenance of a high level of input service quality. As a result, the promotion or maintenance of a high level of input service quality could be appended to the enumeration of ways, identified by William Hansell, that professional city managers add value to the governance and management in the communities they serve.[51]

Actual service outputs or how well services are performed at a particular level of input service quality is something that remains to be compared among cities with different types of executives, government structures, and community features. Contemporary efforts to compare municipal service performance and the lessons from these projects that are applicable to officials in small cities are the topics of the next chapter.

SUMMARY

This chapter explains the distinctions between and importance of input service quality and output service quality. A theoretical framework identified the factors that may affect citizen perceptions of output service quality with the aim of helping local officials to consider sources other than just service performance as possible reasons for popular perceptions of service quality that may be less than desired. Classifying the levels of input service quality is suggested as a strategy for facilitating the identification of potential benchmarking partners and for making later service performance comparisons both fairer and more useful for local officials. Having a professional city manager and an administrative type of local government structure helps to explain why some cities had higher levels of input service quality.

NOTES

1. Robert Behn suggested that determining how public managers can measure achievements in ways that help to increase those achievements is one of the three big questions in contemporary public management. The other two questions concern how public managers can reduce the excess of procedural rules and how managers can motivate people to work toward public purposes. See Robert D. Behn, "The Big Questions in Public Management," *Public Administration Review* 55, no. 4 (1995): 313–24.

2. The need to measure service and program performance is even more compelling in the wake of Governmental Accounting Standards Board (GASB) Statement 34, which now requires communities to net assets and activities, which allows for a greater clarity in matching resources and responsibilities. For additional information on GASB see accounting.rutgers.edu/raw/gasb/repmodel/index.html. Illustrations of the appropriate use of various approaches to organizationwide improvement can be found in Steven Cohen and William Eimicke, *Tools for Innovators: Creative Strategies for Managing Public Sector* Organizations (San Francisco: Jossey-Bass, 1998) and Janet M. Kelly and William C. Rivenbark, *Performance Budgeting for State and Local Government* (Armonk, N.Y.: M. E. Sharpe, 2003).

3. See, for example, Robert L. Lineberry and Edmond P. Fowler, "Reformism and Public Policies in American Cities," *American Political Science Review* 61, no. 3 (1967): 701–16; Roland J. Liebert, "Municipal Functions, Structure, and Expenditures: A Re-analysis of Recent Research," *Social Science Quarterly* 54, no. 1 (1974): 765–83; Theodore J. Stumm and Matthew Corrigan, "City Managers: Do They Promote Efficiency?" *Journal of Urban Affairs* 20, no. 3 (1998): 343–51; and David Morgan and John Pellissero, "Urban Policy: Does Structure Matter?" *American Political Science Review* 74, no. 4 (1980): 999–1006.

4. David N. Ammons, *Municipal Benchmarks: Performance and Establishing Community Standards* (Thousand Oaks, Calif.: Sage, 1996, 2001); David N. Ammons, Charles Coe, and Michael Lombardo, "Performance Comparison Projects in Local Government: Participants' Perspectives," *Public Administration Review* 61, no. 1 (2001): 100–110; and David H. Folz, "Service Quality and Benchmarking the Performance of Municipal Services," *Public Administration Review* 64, no. 2 (2004): 209–20.

5. Theodore H. Poister and Gregory Streib, "Performance Measurement in Municipal Government: Assessing the State of the Practice," *Public Administration Review* 35, no. 3 (2003): 196–205.

6. William C. Rivenbark and Janet M. Kelly, "Management Innovation in Smaller Municipal Government," *State and Local Government Review* 35, no. 3 (2003): 196–205.

7. Joseph S. Wholey and Harry P. Hatry, "The Case for Performance Monitoring," *Public Administration Review* 52, no. 6 (1992): 604–10; Joseph S. Wholey and Kathryn Newcomer, *Improving Government Performance* (San Francisco: Jossey-Bass, 1989); Arie Halachmi, ed., *Performance and Quality Measurement in Government: Issues and Experiences* (Burke, Va.: Chatelaine Press, 1999); and Javier Font, "Quality Measurement in Spanish Municipalities," *Public Productivity and Management Review* 21, no. 1 (1997): 44–55.

8. Eberhard E. Scheuing and William F. Christopher, eds., *The Service Quality Handbook* (New York: American Management Association, 1993).

9. John C. Thomas, *Public Participation in Public Decisions: New Skills and Strategies for Public Managers* (San Francisco: Jossey-Bass, 1995); and David H. Folz, *Survey Research for Public Administration* (Thousand Oaks, Calif.: Sage, 1996).

10. Chuck Chakrapani, *How to Measure Service Quality and Customer Satisfaction: An Informal Field Guide for Tools and Techniques* (Chicago: American Marketing Association, 1998).

11. Kelly and Rivenbark, *Performance Budgeting.* Charlotte, North Carolina is an example of a community that has integrated both organizationwide and programmatic planning.

12. Wendy L. Hassett and Douglas J. Watson, "Citizen Surveys: A Component of the Budgetary Process," *Journal of Public Budgeting, Accounting and Financial Management* 15, no. 4 (2003): 525–42.

13. See Joseph J. Cronin Jr. and Steven Taylor, "SERVPERF Versus SERVQUAL: Reconciling Performance-Based and Perceptions Minus Expectations Measurement of Service Quality," *Journal of Marketing* 58 (January 1994): 125–31; Roland T. Rust and Richard L. Oliver, eds., *Service Quality: New Directions in Theory and Practice* (Thousand Oaks, Calif.: Sage, 1994); and Haksik Lee, Yongki Lee, and Dongkeun Yoo, "The Determinants of Perceived Service Quality and Its Relationship with Satisfaction," *Journal of Services Marketing* 14, no. 3 (2000): 217–31.

14. Rust and Oliver, *Service Quality.*

15. Roger B. Parks, "Linking Objective and Subjective Measures of Performance," *Public Administration Review* 44, no. 2 (1984): 118–27.

16. Richard L. Oliver, "A Cognitive Model of the Antecedents and Consequences of Satisfaction Decisions," *Journal of Marketing Research* 17 (November 1980): 460–69.

17. A. Parasuraman, Valarie A. Zeithaml, and Leonard L. Berry, "Reassessment of Expectations as a Comparison Standard in Measuring Service Quality: Implications for Further Research," *Journal of Marketing* 58 (January 1994): 111–24; Cronin and Taylor, "SERVPERF Versus SERVQUAL," 125–31; Stephen W. Brown and Teresa A. Swartz, "A Gap Analysis of Professional Service Quality," *Journal of Marketing* 53 (April 1989): 92–98; and Emin Babakus and Gregory W. Boller, "An Empirical Assessment of the SERVQUAL Scale," *Journal of Business Research* 24 (1992): 253–68.

18. Salvador Parrado-Diez and Joaquin Ruiz-Lopez, "The Path of Quality in a Spanish Autonomous Agency," *Public Productivity and Management Review* 21, no. 1 (1997): 56–69; and Mik Wisniewski, "Managing Service Quality," *Total Quality Management* 11, no. 6 (2001): 380–88.

19. Cronin and Taylor, "SERVPERF Versus SERVQUAL," 125–31; Lee, Lee, and Yoo, "Determinants of Perceived Service Quality," 217–31. A performance gap may occur when citizens' experience with a service does not meet their needs or expectations. A delivery gap may occur when a disparity exists between what is designed to be provided and what is actually provided by employees. A design gap may occur when the level of input service quality does not correspond with citizens' needs or

preferences. A knowledge gap may occur when local officials do not clearly understand what citizens want, need, or are willing to support financially in terms of the level of input service quality. A communications gap may occur when local officials do not regularly communicate to citizens what service outcomes are produced or achieved with tax revenues.

20. Harry P. Hatry, *Performance Measurement* (Washington, D.C.: The Urban Institute Press, 1999).

21. A. Parasuraman, Valarie A. Zeithaml, and Leonard L. Berry, "Alternative Scales for Measuring Service Quality: A Comparative Assessment Based on Psychometric and Diagnostic Criteria," *Journal of Retailing* 70, no. 3 (1994): 210–30; and Mik Wisniewski and Mike Donnelly, "Measuring Service Quality in the Public Sector: The Potential for SERVQUAL," *Total Quality Management* 7, no. 4 (1996): 357–65.

22. Alexandria Byrsland and Adrienne Curry, "Service Improvements in Public Services Using SERVQUAL," *Managing Service Quality* 11, no. 6 (2001): 389–401; and Mik Wisniewski, "Assessing Customer Satisfaction with Local Authority Services Using SERVQUAL," *Total Quality Management* 12, no. 7–8 (2002): 995–1002.

23. For any service that is not provided to or used by all residents, questions about the quality of a service performance or experience should be preceded by an appropriate screen question that ascertains whether the respondent has used the service during a specific time period. An excellent resource that can help municipalities establish performance targets for service quality for a wide range of services is Ammons, *Municipal Benchmarks*.

24. David N. Ammons, "Performance Measurement and Managerial Thinking," *Public Performance and Management Review*, 25, no. 4 (2002): 344–47.

25. Alfred Ho, "Perceptions of Performance Measurement and the Practice of Performance Reporting by Small Cities," *State and Local Government Review* 35, no. 2 (2003): 161–73.

26. David H. Folz, "Service Quality and Benchmarking," 209–20.

27. See Paul G. Farnham, "The Impact of Government Functional Responsibility on Local Expenditure," *Urban Affairs Quarterly* 22, no. 1 (1986): 151–65; William Lyons, "Reform and Response in American Cities: Structure and Policy Reconsidered," *Social Science Quarterly* 59, no. 2 (1978): 118–32; Roland J. Liebert, *Disintegration and Political Action: The Changing Functions of City Government in America* (New York: Academic Press, 1976); and Liebert, "Municipal Functions, Structure, and Expenditures," 765–83.

28. The Commission on Accreditation for Law Enforcement Agencies, Inc. (CALEA) was established as an independent accrediting authority in 1979 by the four major law enforcement membership associations: International Association of Chiefs of Police (IACP), National Organization of Black Law Enforcement Executives (NOBLE), National Sheriffs' Association (NSA), and Police Executive Research Forum (PERF). For additional information see www.calea.org.

29. Commission on Accreditation for Law Enforcement Agencies, Inc., *Data on Municipal Police Departments Accredited by CALEA,* 2000, at www.calea.org/agcysearch/searchagcy1.cfm (accessed October 7, 2004).

30. Federal Bureau of Investigation, *Crime in the United States, 1999 Uniform Crime Reports* (Washington, D.C.: U.S. Government Printing Office, 1999).

31. For more information about the services provided by the Insurance Services Office, see www.iso.com.

32. Insurance Services Office, at www.iso.com/studies_analyses/ppc_program/docs/p3.html (accessed October 13, 2004).

33. Insurance Services Office, at www.iso.com/studies_analyses/ppc_program/docs/p2.html (accessed October 13, 2004).

34. Charles K. Coe, "A Report on Report Cards," *Public Performance and Management Review* 27, no. 2 (2003): 53–76.

35. Ammons, *Municipal Benchmarks*, 141.

36. During the spring and summer of 2003, Mr. Dennis Gage, ISO manager in the Natural Hazards Mitigation and Risk Decision Services, collected and shared the 1999 PPC ratings and date of each rating for each of the small cities in our study. The PPC ratings for 2000 in table 4.4 that applied to the 45,504 cities in the ISO database was obtained from Insurance Services Office, *ISO's PPC Program* (Jersey City, N.J.: ISO Properties, Inc., 2001).

37. For information on how the ISO's building code effectiveness classifications affect insurance pricing, see Insurance Services Office at www.isomitigation.com/bcegs5.html#q1. The ISO also employs two additional categories. A rating of "99" means that a city is unclassified because its building code enforcement does not meet minimum criteria and is therefore ineligible for BCEGS insurance discounts. A rating of "98" is reserved for Florida cities that refuse to participate in the BCEGS program. All cities in participating states had their ratings assigned by the end of 2000.

38. Dennis Gage (ISO Manager, Natural Hazards Mitigations and Risk Decision Services, Insurance Services Office), telephone discussion with author, April 4, 2003.

39. Data obtained at the U.S. Environmental Protection Agency website, http://www.epa.gov/epaoswer/nonhw/muncpl/recycle.htm#Figures (accessed October 12, 2004).

40. David H. Folz, "Service Quality and Benchmarking," 209–20. The quality of service framework for recycling programs presented in this article indicated that the two most important dimensions of input service quality are recycling convenience and scope of targeted materials.

41. The relationships among population size, metro status, median income, and service quality level are statistically significant at the .05 level. The respective gamma values for each relationship are population = −.487; metro status = −.303; median income = −.216. High school graduation rate was not related to the overall service quality measure.

42. The relationships between type of chief executive, type of local government structure, and service quality level are statistically significant at the .05 level. The gamma values are −.228 and −.144 for type of executive and type of structure, respectively.

43. Since the variables are measured at the ordinal level, elaboration analysis was used to examine the relationships among type of executive, type of government, and input service quality within the categories of the population and median household income variables. For more information on the elaboration model see Daniel F. Cham-

bliss and Russell Schutt, *Making Sense of the Social World: Methods of Investigation* (Thousand Oaks, Calif.: Sage, 2003).

44. For cities with populations between 15,000 and 25,000, the relationship between input service quality and type of executive was statistically significant and had a gamma value of –.314. Elaboration logic indicates that this finding specifies the conditions (the population group) under which the type of executive (having a city manager) matters in terms of input service quality.

45. For cities with median household incomes below the group mean, the relationship between input service quality and type of executive was statistically significant and had a gamma value of –.198, which indicates that only in the less wealthy cities does having a city manager appear to be related to having a higher level of input service quality.

46. The relationship between input service quality and type of local government structure was statistically significant and had a gamma value of –.219 for cities with a population of 15,000 or more. This indicates that the cities in this population class with a high level of input service quality were more likely to have an administrative type of local government structure.

47. The relationship between input service quality and type of local government structure was statistically significant and had a gamma value of –.206 for cities with median household incomes above the group mean.

48. See James H. Svara, *Official Leadership in the City: Patterns of Conflict and Cooperation* (Oxford: Oxford University Press, 1990); H. George Fredrickson, *The Spirit of Public Administration* (San Francisco: Jossey-Bass, 1996); and Robert S. Montjoy and Douglas J. Watson, "A Case for Reinterpreted Dichotomy of Politics and Administration as a Professional Standard in Council-Manager Government," *Public Administration Review* 55, no. 3 (1995): 231–39.

49. See Liebert, "Municipal Functions, Structure, and Expenditures," 765–83; Stumm and Corrigan, "City Managers: Do They Promote Efficiency?" 343–51; and Morgan and Pellissero, "Urban Policy," 999–1006.

50. Chester A. Newland, "Managing from the Future in Council-Manager Government," in *Ideal and Practice in Council-Manager Government*, ed. H. George Frederickson, 263–83 (Washington, D.C.: ICMA Press, 1994).

51. William J. Hansell Jr., "Council-Manager Government: Alive and Leading Today's Best-Managed Communities," *National Civic Review* 90, no. 1 (2001): 41–43. Hansell observed that management professionals also add value to the communities they serve by establishing policy and service delivery strategies on the basis of need rather than demand, emphasizing long-term community interests, promoting equity and fairness, recognizing the interconnectedness of policies, and advancing broad and inclusive citizen participation.

5

Measuring and Comparing Municipal Service Performance

Providing public services in an era of increased public scrutiny and pressure for operational accountability requires prudent local officials to monitor service quality and the results achieved with local tax dollars.[1] For some time, public administration scholars and practitioners have recognized the potential benefits of an ongoing process of performance monitoring as well as some of the potential problems that can occur when the wrong things get measured. Overall, it is fair to say that a consensus exists in the public administration community that it is better to measure service performance than not to measure it.

However, anyone with experience in measuring service performance understands that often what gets measured is what gets done. Consequently, considerable thought must be given to the types of measures adopted, always with an eye to anticipating possible unintended consequences or behaviors that various measures might engender. The mistakes made in the past have become today's anecdotes and urban legends about good measurement intentions gone awry. One example is the community that adopted "tickets written per officer" as a measure of police performance only to be flooded with complaints from a highly aggravated citizenry. Another example is the city that adopted "tons of asphalt used per employee" for pothole repairs only to learn that repair crews were digging cutouts wider and deeper than necessary to "improve" their performance ratings.

Such anecdotes only underscore the importance of embedding performance measurement within integrated organization-wide and program-level planning efforts that align performance measures with the mission of, goals for, and decisions about local service policies.[2] A number of resources can help local officials in small communities integrate planning and decision making, and they describe the considerations involved in performance measurement.[3] This chapter examines several key aspects of contemporary efforts to capture and report comparative performance data for several vital local services. The aim is to highlight what has been learned from municipal benchmarking efforts that can help to advance the practice of performance measurement and performance comparison among small communities.

This chapter describes the principle features of five U.S. municipal benchmarking projects; the types of measures they employ to compare service performance; the challenges and problems encountered in trying to compare performance; and the implications of these comparative performance experiences that should inform efforts among small communities that want to launch, refine, or advance a performance measurement program. The particular value of measuring input service quality in the context of a benchmarking project also is reviewed.

There are a number of excellent resources, including professional organizations, that offer a surfeit of information about how to choose, implement, and use performance measures.[4] These resources provide a good starting point for learning how to "do" performance measurement. For instance, one national survey of finance officers in small cities indicates that only 17 percent require performance measurement by some or all local programs, 39 percent do not collect and report performance measures systematically, and 44 percent do not use performance measurement at all.[5] Among the small cities that use performance measures systematically, the most commonly used are workload and efficiency measures, which typically are reported annually and compared with a peg that may be a previous point in time, another unit in the same organization, a preestablished target, or an existing standard.[6] Very few cities attempt to compare their performance with that attained by other communities. Yet there is much that officials in small communities can learn from cities that have had more experience in measuring performance, especially those that have participated in municipal benchmarking projects. That is the rationale for focusing on the experiences of contemporary municipal benchmarking projects.

Systematic comparisons of municipal performance in the United States are not widespread. Why do not more cities provide their citizens with information about how their city performs compared to other jurisdictions? Two reasons appear to be paramount: practical constraints and political risk. From a practical standpoint, local officials in small towns who aspire to be numbered among or recognized as belonging to the cadre of top service performers often find that a search for communities that employ measures of outcomes and service effectiveness useful for comparison purposes yields a pitifully small sample. In addition, the most common types of measures that cities report are workload or output indicators, and these have limited utility for comparing performance.[7]

From a political standpoint, some local officials may fear what service comparisons might show. Comfort with the status quo can be a strong motivator for not wanting to deal with the pressure for change and improvement that could stem from an explicit performance comparison with another community. The "uniqueness" argument that what the cities do or how they do it is incomparable has been used by some local officials to deflect intercity comparisons. However, this argument has been discredited in light of the findings discussed in chapter 4 and other evidence that shows it is possible to identify organizations with comparable levels of service. It is also quite possible to compare how well they deliver services.[8] More cities in the future may consider participating in cooperative efforts to collect and share service performance statistics in order to understand how their performance stacks up against that of other jurisdictions. The Governmental Accounting and Standards Board (GASB), for example, suggests that cities should, where possible, compare their performance with other jurisdictions.[9]

What is it about a benchmarking project that promises to advance what we know about the art and science of performance measurement and that can help to inform existing or planned service performance measurement efforts? For one thing, nothing better exposes the value of or limitations inherent in a particular performance measure than attempting to use that measure to assess how one city's service operation compares with another community's. Service managers have a keen sense of whether a particular measure captures some aspect of their departmental or unit service performance. Any measure proposed to be used as a means to compare performance across jurisdictions is like striking flint; it is bound to ignite any concerns about its validity, accuracy, and collection burden. Performance measures that survive this "trial by fire," especially those that are refined by years of collective experience, are worth consideration by other communities.

In addition, we live in an era of management practice that prizes continual performance improvement. It is unclear what level of performance for a service is realistically achievable. How good is good enough? Intercity performance comparisons can help to chart the boundaries of the attainable. Finally, performance comparisons promise to advance the still largely enigmatic process of connecting high performance with particular local resources, policies, and practices. In other words, there is still much to be learned about how cities can replicate the high performance levels achieved by some communities. Before reviewing the U.S. municipal benchmarking experiences, it is important to clarify several key concepts related to benchmarking and measuring performance.

APPROACHES TO PERFORMANCE BENCHMARKING

Benchmarking is just one strategy that can help local officials in their quest to improve the performance of local services.[10] Benchmarking is a term that has been adapted from professional land surveyors and involves a comparison of at least two data points on a measure of performance.[11] One of those points is specified as the benchmark or reference point that local officials can use to determine how their service performance compares to the benchmark. The difference between the benchmark performance standard (or target) and a city's performance level is often referred to as a performance gap. The challenge for local officials is to determine why a gap exists and then to identify possible actions or strategies that can help to improve the city's service performance to bring it more in line with the desired performance benchmark.

By itself, benchmarking is not a magic bullet for solving performance issues. It is merely one tool or process that local officials can use to analyze service performance in a systematic way with the idea of determining what things about a local service can be or need to be changed to help improve performance so that it corresponds more closely to some desired performance level.[12] The value of a benchmarking effort depends on local managers choosing the form of benchmarking that best matches the purpose or goal for establishing performance benchmarks in the first place and then selecting the right benchmark for comparison purposes.

There are four approaches to performance benchmarking, the distinct purposes of which are summarized in table 5.1. The four most prevalent forms of benchmarking in public administration are continuous process improvement, performance targets, corporate style, and comparative performance statistics.[13]

Continuous process improvement is perhaps the most widely used form of benchmarking, mainly because it is the least burdensome from an analytical standpoint. Local officials simply compare their own city's service performance, over some period of time, using the same measures. The idea is to encourage managers and employee service teams to focus on ideas for changing or modifying the ways that a service is provided and that might help to improve service efficiency, effectiveness. or results. As part of a continuing effort to enhance performance, local managers regularly evaluate the potential of ideas for improving performance, such as how work and workers are organized, trained, deployed, and supervised; the merits of different technologies, materials, or support systems; or how employee performance is measured and rewarded. Obviously, there is only so much performance improvement that can be attained at a given resource level after implementing the best ideas for improvement. Performance plateaus are common. However, the continuing

Table 5.1. Approaches to Performance Benchmarking

Approach	Purpose
Continuous Process Improvement	An internal comparison of current and previous performance with the aim of identifying opportunities to improve a service delivery process
Performance Targets	A comparison of current performance against a preestablished internal performance target or an external target derived from a similar organization or industry standard with the aim of improving a service process or monitoring progress toward achieving a performance goal
Corporate Style	A comparison of current performance with a top-performing comparable service counterpart with the aim of identifying best practices and policies that can help to improve service efficiency and effectiveness
Comparative Performance Statistics	Comparing current service performance with the benchmark performance achieved by other cities with high levels of service efficiency or effectiveness

focus on raising the "performance bar" helps to justify requests for additional resources once those plateaus are reached.

Performance targets as benchmarks can be derived from an internal assessment of previous performance trends; from external standards based on achievements by a similar city; or from a standard published by a relevant professional, trade, or industry source. Performance targets are especially useful for those service functions where internal control over the success of programs is high.[14] Ammons has provided an indispensable resource for local officials who wish to consider these municipal service benchmarks as a way to monitor the performance of service operations.[15] A performance target for police patrol, for example, might involve a 40 percent figure for the proportion of a shift that an officer is available for proactive patrol.[16] A performance target for a recycling service might be a 33 percent diversion rate.[17] The principal drawback with using performance targets as benchmarks is that they are somewhat arbitrary. Linkage to a truly comparable service operation in another city is tenuous, which means that local officials have little or no guidance about how to improve service practices to attain a desired performance target.

Corporate style benchmarking is a more extensive process that is rooted in the experience of private sector efforts to identify and import best practices to

improve performance.[18] This approach requires local officials to determine
which services or programs are most likely to benefit from an external comparison, measure the level of current service performance, search and find a
suitable and agreeable benchmarking partner, ascertain the comparability of
performance measures, collect and analyze performance data, and identify
what practices or policies can be adapted that appear to have promise for clos-
ing a performance gap.[19]

In this approach to benchmarking, public officials compare their jurisdiction's service performance statistics to those of an appropriate municipal coun-
terpart, with the goal of understanding how they can close the gap between
where they are and where they want to be.[20] The idea is to adapt particular policies and practices used by top-performing jurisdictions in an effort to realize a
comparable level of performance. By identifying a high-performing city that
offers a comparable service, the idea is that local officials should be able to
adapt some of the community's "best" practices to achieve a similar level of
performance.

The corporate approach to benchmarking requires a significant investment
of time, effort, and analytical skill. Done carefully, it can result in specific recommendations for how a service process might be changed to attain a higher
performance level. In practice, the most significant challenge inherent in this
approach is actually finding a comparable service operation provided by
another city that employs the desired performance measures and that can
attribute its high performance to specific policies or practices.

The use of *comparative performance statistics* for benchmarking purposes
is an approach that emerged in the 1990s. It is similar in form to corporate
benchmarking except that in practice it is the product of a cooperative effort
among cities, the participants in which agree on common performance metrics
and processes for collecting, verifying, and sharing performance information on particular services.[21] One of the first national comparative performance projects was led by the ICMA's Center for Performance Measurement,
which collects performance data from ninety-two cities and thirty-eight counties on fifteen different services.[22] Four other state or regional projects involve
cooperative efforts among localities to collect and share performance information or the results obtained from innovative practices. An example of the
latter is the Northwest Municipal Conference, which involves forty-six suburban communities and four townships located northwest of Chicago. State-
level municipal benchmarking projects include the North Carolina Local
Government Performance Measurement Project, the South Carolina Municipal Benchmarking Project, and the Tennessee Municipal Benchmarking Project. The key features of each of these projects are discussed in a subsequent
section.

TYPES OF MEASURES USED IN ASSESSING SERVICE PERFORMANCE

One source of confusion about performance measures is the lack of consistency in the use of terminology in the literature on this subject. There are at least six different types of measures that are relevant for measuring service performance. Among the comparative municipal benchmarking projects, information is collected on all of these types of measures with the exception of productivity indicators. The six types of measures germane to measuring performance are:

- inputs,
- workload or outputs,
- efficiency,
- effectiveness or outcomes,
- quality, and
- productivity.

Figure 5.1 shows how these types of measures are related to the logic of a typical municipal service or program and provides examples of the different types of measures.

Inputs are the resources, demands, and constraints that are dedicated to or consumed by the provision of a service or program. Resources include the number of employees; the amount of money or budget size; and the array of equipment, facilities, utilities, and materials used or consumed in the process of producing outputs. For most public services, the single most expensive resource input is typically the cost of labor. Demands and expectations refer to the volume of requests for a service or the number of persons, clients, households, businesses, or entities that require, demand, or need a particular service. This information is useful for managers who need to know how service demands and expectations may be changing so that adjustments in resources can be made. Expectations refer specifically to the level of input quality that recipients prefer or are willing to support for a particular service. Constraints refer to the legal, regulatory, or political parameters that characterize the environment in which a service is provided. Input measures by themselves do not tell us anything about service performance. However, data on the input volumes, together with other community profile information, are necessary to compute other indicators of performance.

Output or workload measures indicate the amount of work performed; the volume of services provided during a particular period of time; or the quantity of calls, reports, or requests that require some response, action, or attention by service personnel. These measures *only* tell us how much is done or needs to

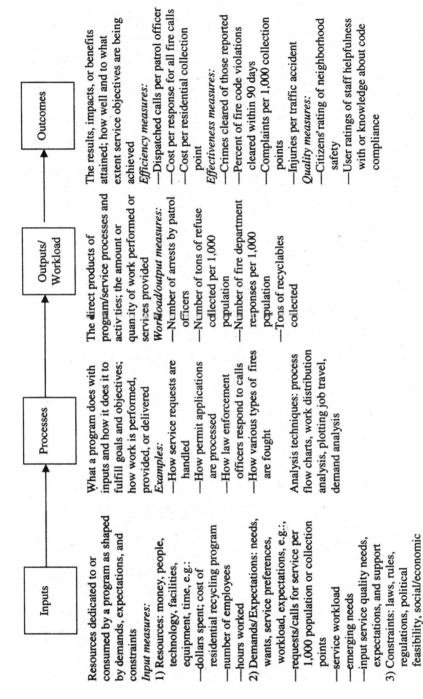

Inputs	Processes	Outputs/Workload	Outcomes

Resources dedicated to or consumed by a program as shaped by demands, expectations, and constraints

Input measures:

1) Resources: money, people, technology, facilities, equipment, time, e.g.:
   —dollars spent; cost of residential recycling program
   —number of employees
   —hours worked
2) Demands/Expectations: needs, wants, service preferences, workload, expectations, e.g.:
   —requests/calls for service per 1,000 population or collection points
   —service workload
   —emerging needs
   —input service quality needs, expectations, and support
3) Constraints: laws, rules, regulations, political feasibility, social/economic conditions

What a program does with inputs and how it does it to fulfill goals and objectives; how work is performed, provided, or delivered

Examples:
   —How service requests are handled
   —How permit applications are processed
   —How law enforcement officers respond to calls
   —How various types of fires are fought

Analysis techniques: process flow charts, work distribution analysis, plotting job travel, demand analysis

The direct products of program/service processes and activities; the amount or quantity of work performed or services provided

Workload/output measures:
   —Number of arrests by patrol officers
   —Number of tons of refuse collected per 1,000 population
   —Number of fire department responses per 1,000 population
   —Tons of recyclables collected

The results, impacts, or benefits attained; how well and to what extent service objectives are being achieved

Efficiency measures:
   —Dispatched calls per patrol officer
   —Cost per response for all fire calls
   —Cost per residential collection point

Effectiveness measures:
   —Crimes cleared of those reported
   —Percent of fire code violations cleared within 90 days
   —Complaints per 1,000 collection points
   —Injuries per traffic accident

Quality measures:
   —Citizens' rating of neighborhood safety
   —User ratings of staff helpfulness with or knowledge about code compliance

Figure 5.1.   Service/Program Logic and the Types of Measures Used in Performance Assessment

be done, not how efficiently or how well it is done. Nonetheless, these measures are useful for comparing how workload may be changing over time. For example, workload measures can indicate how many service requests, calls, or cases were served, processed, or handled. Often these measures are expressed as a ratio of work accomplished per unit of some standard such as per officer, per 1,000 population, or per worker. Information for these measures is fairly easy to collect, therefore city officials are sometimes inclined to accumulate a lot of it.

Collecting multiple measures is usually wise. However, when used improperly, there is a high risk of creating unintended consequences. Perverse incentives can be created if workload measures are used as exclusive indicators of employee performance. "Tickets written per officer" or "tons of asphalt used per road crew employee" are the classic examples previously described. Nonetheless, workload or output information has value for supervisors and managers who need to know how the volume of work varies and what factors explain or account for those variations. For example, output variations may be the result of changes in the size or character of the population or clientele, changes in the qualitative nature or difficulty of the problems or needs being addressed, or a difference in the level of effort expended by employees.

While some authors reserve the term *outcomes* for indicators of service effectiveness only, we apply this label broadly to measures of service efficiency, effectiveness, quality, and productivity. The rationale for doing so is that each of these indicators measures a distinct aspect of a result or outcome attained or achieved by a service or program. Moreover, each outcome indicator has utility for the different kinds of decisions managers may need to make about a particular service result.

Efficiency measures express a relationship between outputs and inputs, typically the amount of work performed per unit of resource input. Unit costs, such as cost per residential collection point, are among the most common type of efficiency measure, but many other efficiency measures are possible. Examples include tons of materials recycled per number of full-time collection personnel, police costs per full-time equivalent (FTE), and cost per fire call response.

Measures of efficiency, like all performance measures, must be employed carefully to avoid creating perverse behaviors or unintended consequences. Unit costs for a service may change for reasons that have nothing to do with variations in employee effort. Fuel, material, and supply costs may increase and affect the unit cost of work performed. Clearly, these are outside the control of employees and supervisors. So why collect efficiency measures? Their value lies in alerting managers to possible cost or effort issues when the measure of service efficiency departs substantially from a standard, target, or benchmark or when compared to the same type of service during the same period of time for another entity. For example, if the unit costs for a curbside recycling service provided by municipal employees are substantially higher than the costs incurred by a private firm that provides a similar service during the same time period, then the difference in efficiency should prompt managers to investigate the reasons for that difference and to pursue strategies to increase service efficiency.

Effectiveness measures should quantify the extent to which service or program performance objectives are achieved. These indicators can provide local officials with the most meaningful kind of information about service performance, but simultaneously they are among the most difficult to quantify. First, to measure the effectiveness of a service, local officials must have clearly specified service objectives. While identifying local objectives for some services such as law enforcement, fire protection, or solid waste collection and recycling is fairly straightforward, this task is more difficult for services that are inherently more complex, have multiple objectives or have ambiguous goals such as "providing a decent living environment for low income residents."[23] For example, it is fairly easy to reach agreement about measuring law enforcement effectiveness through indicators such as crimes cleared or rate of accidents with injuries.[24] It is much more difficult to agree on a measure for what constitutes a decent living environment. Likewise, it is easier to establish an outcome target for law enforcement that might involve, for example, a 2 percent decrease in accidents with injuries. This result might be achieved by stricter enforcement of traffic laws. How does one set a goal for an ill-defined, difficult to quantify outcome? This is one reason most municipal benchmarking projects focus on performance measures for "hard" rather than "soft" local services. Nevertheless, some progress is being made to devise measures for some of the more difficult to quantify service outcomes.[25]

Quality measures of service outcomes, as described in the previous chapter, indicate what citizens who receive or experience a service think about the performance of that service in terms of whether it meets (or exceeds) their needs or expectations. Good measures of output service quality should tap what citizens think about any applicable dimensions of the service that relate to reliability, interaction with municipal employees, the adequacy of physical facilities, and opinions about service policies. The most commonly used method for obtaining feedback on output service quality is through survey research. As pointed out in the previous chapter, however, the value of these data for informing management decisions depends on careful study of the multiple points in a service process at which a gap or difference may occur that might account for why citizens' perceptions of service quality are that it does not meet or exceed their needs, preferences, or expectations.

Productivity measures can provide very useful information for local managers, but they also are rarely used indicators of service outcomes. In fact, none of the existing municipal benchmarking projects employ them. Productivity measures combine indicators of efficiency and effectiveness into a single number. For example, suppose recycling collection crews are responsible for properly separating, by type, recyclable materials that citizens set out at the curb. If cost per ton of recyclable materials measures efficiency, and number of tons of materials properly segregated (not contaminated with mixed materials) measures effectiveness, then cost per ton of properly segregated recyclable materials (by type) might serve as a measure of recycling service productivity. The costs for all material tonnage are included in the numerator, but only the properly segregated tons get counted in the denominator. The utility of productivity measures is that they have the potential to encourage both efficiency and effectiveness.

MUNICIPAL BENCHMARKING PROJECTS

The brief summaries of the four municipal benchmarking projects presented in this section describe the number and type of cities involved, their organization and operation, the types of services for which performance data are collected, and the nature of any effort to identify best practices. A subsequent section discusses the lessons learned from these benchmarking projects that can help small town officials with decisions about how to measure and benchmark the performance of their municipal services. The fundamental value of each of these benchmarking efforts lies in their potential to suggest opportunities for service performance improvement.

A detailed summary of the types of community data, service profile information, and performance measures used by the ICMA, North Carolina, South Carolina, and Tennessee benchmarking projects is presented in appendix A. The diversity of measures chosen by local officials in each of the respective benchmarking efforts reflects their judgment about which indicators of service inputs, outputs, and outcomes are most appropriate for their service operations.

The ICMA Benchmarking Project

The International City/County Management Association's (ICMA) Center for Performance Measurement, created in 1997, continues the work begun in 1994 by the Comparative Performance Measurement Consortium, which was composed of a group of managers in forty-four large cities and counties from across the United States who were interested in measuring, comparing, and improving local services.[26] The Center for Performance Measurement has expanded upon this seminal municipal benchmarking effort and now performs staff functions that include collecting, cleaning, and reporting performance data on fifteen different services for a dozen counties and some eighty cities, the mean population of which is over 300,000.[27] Among the participating cities, only four have populations of less than 25,000, and only 16 percent have a mayor-council form of government, which is substantially below the national proportion of 43.6 percent of cities with this form. The Center charges an annual fee of $5,000 per jurisdiction and there is an additional, one-time training fee of $3,900 for new enrollees.[28]

For each service, the ICMA Center for Performance Measurement, with the assistance of participants, defines the concepts and measures used for each particular service. The participating local governments agree to adhere to these definitions even if local practice or preferences differ. An important task for the Center's staff is to clean the data submitted. This involves checking statistical outliers and verifying questionable data points with participants. Questionable data that are not verified are removed from the performance data set.

However, an issue that appears to remain only partially resolved for the scores of participants is the extent to which data verification reconciles desired versus actual use of the same definitions in data collection and reporting. For example, in the FY 2002 data collection effort, the arson clearance rate ranged from 1.2 to 50.0 percent.[29] In another instance, the operating and maintenance cost of refuse collection per refuse collection account ranged from about $15 to almost $160.[30] The explanatory information provided with these data notes that one of the possible reasons for the variation among jurisdictions could be the difference in how arson fires are defined and reported among jurisdictions or the way that cities allocate costs between their collection and disposal budgets.

The cities that participate in the ICMA municipal benchmarking project receive feedback in the form of data, graphs, and charts for their city and others on all of the performance measures. These resources enable local officials to compare their own performance across time and with other participants. The Center provides whisker graphs that depict a city's performance compared to the median and various percentiles on each performance measure.

The Center for Performance Measurement does not grade or rank communities on overall performance. To do so is inconsistent with the organization's stated mission to assist communities in improving the efficiency and effectiveness of services. Moreover, the ICMA suggests that participants may disproportionately represent cities that are above average service performers and include local officials who have an extraordinary level of interest in service improvements.[31] What ICMA expects local officials to do is to consider using the results achieved by higher performing cities as performance targets for specific departments, contact colleagues in those cities to learn what they may be doing differently, and consider whether any of their practices might be adapted for local use.[32]

The Northwest Municipal Conference Projects

The Northwest Municipal Conference (NWMC) is a council of government (COG) comprising forty-six cities and four townships located in the northwestern Chicago suburbs. About one-half of the participating cities have populations under 25,000. In contrast to ICMA's national benchmarking project, the NWMC employs an entirely different approach to identifying best practices. In conjunction with a private contractor (City Tech USA, Inc.), the NWMC offers subscribers an online software program called the Dynamic Government Performance Measurement. This project, in a nascent stage of development, collects a limited number of input, output, and efficiency measures from cities that subscribe to particular software modules for different services. These modules include police, fire, community planning, and public works. The objective is to provide participants with performance data that can be compared horizontally or within a group of cities that possess similar attributes (e.g., population, income, geographic location, etc.), also known as "comparables."[33]

Ostensibly, local officials can use this information to track performance trends in their own jurisdiction and to analyze "what if" scenarios that may involve issues related to the relationship between workload changes and personnel requirements. For example, the program may help local administrators determine rational solutions to scenarios such as, if the number of permit applications increases by 10 percent, how many more building inspectors are required? The software employed appears to be limited to measures of service inputs, outputs, and efficiency. There is no publicly released report on performance data, and the NWMC staff do not rate or rank cities based on their service performance.[34]

In a separate but companion program, an NWMC Best Practices Committee identifies best practices based on submissions by member communities. A best practice is one that is cost-effective and results in reduced citizen complaints or a higher level of service.[35] From among the annual submissions by communities that belong to the NWMC, several practices may be chosen as recipients of a Best Practices, Bright Idea Award. In 2003, for example, one small community received the award for a "Crossing Guard Communication System" that equipped twenty-one civilian crossing guards with old cellular phones donated by village residents so that guards could call 911 in the event of an emergency. The surplus phones donated were given to domestic abuse shelters and to area social workers, extending the benefit of the donated cellular phones.[36]

This effort to identify best practices spans several services and functions, including public safety, communication and technology, health and human services, human resources and education, infrastructure, and economic development and revenue enhancement. Examples of innovative ideas or best practices implemented by some of the suburban communities in these areas include:

- a residential and commercial security survey program implemented by village of Wilmette police in which trained officers conduct thorough exterior and interior security inspections that result in a report of findings and suggested security remedies;
- a reciprocal agreement for incident duty coverage implemented by the village of Niles that helps to reduce or eliminate overtime costs and extra staffing; command officers from different fire districts agree to respond to calls when a community's command officer is on furlough, on sick leave, or absent for some other reason;
- an administrative adjudication program by the village of Skokie that diverts noncriminal, nonmoving violations of local ordinances from circuit court to a hearing officer for adjudication with the aim of improving speed, convenience, and efficiency of case processing; and
- a new employee video orientation developed by the village of Hoffman Estates that introduces new employees to the city's organizational structure and scope of services and operations.[37]

In effect, the NWMC serves as a clearinghouse for sharing information about ideas and practices that member communities believe have improved their service performance. The emphasis is on belief, since evidence based on performance measures is not required. It is up to local officials in each city to decide if any of the ideas developed by their peers have merit for local application.

The North Carolina Benchmarking Project

The North Carolina Local Government Performance Measurement Project began in 1995 when fourteen large cities and counties in the state agreed to compare performance and cost data for selected governmental services. Originally, seven cities and seven counties participated, but the third phase of the project involved only fourteen cities with populations that ranged in size from 26,444 to 580,597 with a mean size of 140,678. For FY 2003–2004, the project was to include an additional city with a population under 25,000. Participating cities are charged a flat fee of $10,000.

Policy decisions about what to measure, how to measure it, and how to assure accuracy and comparability in data are made by members of a steering committee comprising a representative from each participating city. The project is managed by staff at the University of North Carolina Institute of Government, who collect and clean the data and issue annual reports on service performance for nine services: asphalt maintenance and repair, building inspections, emergency communications, fire services, fleet maintenance, household recycling, police services, residential refuse collection, and yard waste/leaf collection.[38] Members of the Steering Committee track how the cost and performance data are used by cities to improve services and how this information is linked to local budgetary processes.[39]

Project staff with the UNC Institute of Government engage in an extensive data review and cleaning process with the city service managers, who complete the service profile spreadsheets, and the city budget or finance officers, who complete the accounting spreadsheets.[40] After review of the draft report by local officials and members of the project Steering Committee, a final report is prepared and distributed that compares each city's results on each service output or outcome measure with the relevant mean for all cities involved in the project that submitted data. Data are collected on input, output, and outcome measures of efficiency and effectiveness. Graphs for each measure are provided for the current year and two previous years so that trends over time can be discerned.

Like the ICMA project, the North Carolina benchmarking effort does not rank cities on any performance measure. Rather, the final report provides explanatory information that describes the level and process of service delivery employed by each city for each service and lists several factors that appear to explain at least some of the differences in service cost and performance among the fourteen cities involved in the project.[41] For example, factors found to affect residential refuse collection cost and performance for at least some of the cities were the collection cycle, size of crews, type of equipment used, privatization, distance to landfill/transfer station, and fee policies. For police services, factors that affected performance included demographics, community policing policies, use of incident-based reporting, vehicle take-home policy, beat structure, and use of special units. For fire services, factors that helped to explain cost and performance included the number of engine companies, the number of fire code violations, and the ISO rating.[42]

With these indications about the factors that may affect cost and performance, local officials may contact their cohorts to exchange additional information that may help to identify why particular practices may contribute to lower service costs or higher performance levels. In addition, the UNC Institute of Government hosts an annual meeting of benchmarking project participants and other municipal officials at which information is exchanged about which practices and policies seem to be helping or not helping to solve various service performance problems and issues.[43]

The South Carolina Benchmarking Project

With assistance from staff at the University of South Carolina's Institute for Public Service and Policy Research, a pilot performance benchmarking project was initiated in June 1996 when eleven cities agreed to collect and report performance data for fire, police, and solid waste services.[44] The project has since expanded to include seventeen cities and one additional municipal service, parks and recreation.[45] Nine of these cities have populations under 25,000, and fourteen of the participating cities have a council-manager form of government. Data are collected on input, output, and outcomes that include efficiency, effectiveness, and quality measures.

As in the North Carolina project, a steering committee composed of managers and administrators from the participating communities provides leadership and direction for the project. In addition, service committees composed of municipal line managers are responsible for developing standards for service profiles and performance measures. The members of these committees are the agents responsible for collecting and reviewing the relevant performance information for their cities. In addition, a finance committee composed of the finance directors/officers from each city is responsible for implementing the cost accounting model, assisting members of the other line committees in designing cost measures, and ensuring consistency in measuring direct and indirect costs. Information on service costs follows an agreed upon indirect cost plan, and data on measures of service quality are derived from a biennial telephone survey of a random sample of two hundred citizens in each municipality.[46]

In the 2001 performance report for the South Carolina Municipal Benchmarking Project, the latest available at this writing, the staff identified several key indicators that distinguished service performance among cities. Table 5.2 summarizes the range of performance on three such factors found to be related to police, fire, and solid waste services, respectively, for the nine cities in the project that have populations of less than 25,000.

Interpretation of these performance data should begin by recognizing the type of information that each measure represents. For example, "Crime rate per 1,000 population" is a workload measure for police (see appendix A) that indicates the relative volume of crimes reported in each city. Police response time is an efficiency measure, and the clearance rate for crimes is a measure

Table 5.2. Performance Profile on Selected Indicators for Small Cities in the South Carolina Benchmarking Project, FY 2001

City	Pop.	Police — Crime Rate per 1,000	Police — Response Time	Police — Clearance Rate UCR Crimes I (%)	Fire — Number of Fires/1,000 Pop. Resid.	Fire — Number of Fires/1,000 Pop. Comrcl	Fire — Response Time Dispatch to Arrival	Fire — Clearance Rate (%) Fire Code Violations	Solid Waste — Cost per Resident. Collection Point	Recycling — Cost per Resident. Collection Point	Recycling — Percent Waste Reduction (recycling)
York	6,985	80.63	5:00	72.87	2.06		4:00	43	$48.35	$22.27	12.61
Lancaster	8,177	168.40	4:30	41.10	3.06		2:09	68	$109.23		
Georgetown	8,950	94.70		28.62	2.60	1.7		67	$178.67	$12.92	8.84
N. Myrtle Beach	10,974	27.41		15.67	1.30	1.00			$38.53	$11.92	10.31
Clemson	11,939	39.68		26.09					$74.61	$37.88	15.97
Orangeburg	12,765	94.33	4:00	16.61	2.00	0.53	2:32	91	$58.14	$31.37	4.44
Beaufort	12,950	70.04	6:34	16.10	1.54	0.47	2:35	97	$80.91	$32.60	18.87
North Augusta	17,574	48.37	4:47	15.06	1.63	0.45	6:29	100	$49.29	$37.32	22.78
Myrtle Beach	22,759	99.35			0.93	0.43	3:40	86	$46.17	$16.51	27.37
Means		80.32	5:00	29.01	1.89	.776	3:40	78.86	$75.99	$25.35	15.13

of police service effectiveness. The city of York, for example, has a crime rate and mean response time that are near the means for these small cities, but it has the highest clearance rate. Supervisors in other police departments might want to know why York was able to attain this high value on service effectiveness. Does it have something to do with the types of crimes committed, available departmental resources, or perhaps how resources are deployed or organized to fight crime and to investigate cases?

Likewise, fire chiefs might want to know why Beaufort and Orangeburg were able to clear almost all of their fire code violations and sustain a rapid time of response between dispatch and arrival. Are they using the same definitions of code violations? How are these departments staffed? What resources do they have to deploy? Are there certain community features that help to explain these performance levels or are there practices or policies used that other communities might find useful for elevating service performance? The information collected by the benchmarking project staff on community features, demographics, and service processes helps to point to issues that can to be investigated further by other local officials interested in the results.

The avowed purpose of the performance reports published by the University of South Carolina Institute for Public Service and Policy is to provide a management tool for participating local officials. These reports do not attempt to rank cities on any of the service performance indicators. Staff for the project find little support for such rankings among the officials of the participating cities.[47]

Local officials are encouraged to compare their city's results on the performance measures with those attained by other cities of comparable size and to contact the service managers of those jurisdictions to learn more about their service operations and practices.[48] Information sharing about "best practices" is generally informal and takes the form of discussions, for example, about whether one city's use of an automated trash collection vehicle operated by single staff improves efficiency and citizen satisfaction with the service.

To prompt discussions about possible best practices, staff for the project identify in the published performance reports those variables that appear to be related and unrelated to (not necessarily the cause of) municipal differences on various performance measures. For example, staff analyses found that the only variable that was significantly related to the efficiency and quality measures for refuse collection was the fully automated one-person collection vehicle.[49] For the measures of citizen perceptions of safety, the USC staff found an inverse relationship between the number of neighborhood crime watch programs in a city and the proportion of citizens who feel safe, speculating that these watch programs are a response to a crime problem that causes citizens to feel unsafe in the first place.[50] For fire protection services, the staff found that the level of citizen satisfaction with local fire protection service is higher among those communities that offer more fire prevention education programs and have a larger number of residents who attend those programs.[51] Local officials are expected to consider the feasibility of adapting some or all aspects of the practices that appear to be related to desirable results on the indicators of service performance.

The Tennessee Benchmarking Project

Modeled after the process employed by the North Carolina project, the Tennessee Municipal Benchmarking Project, staffed by the University of Tennessee Municipal Technical Advisory Service (MTAS), was launched in 2001 with nine participating cities, a number that grew to twelve mostly medium-sized cities by 2004. The population of cities that participated in FY 2003 ranged from 23,120 to 173,890 and had a mean size of about 63,000 people. Only one community had a 2003 certified population of less than 25,000 people. Six of the participating cities have a mayor-council form with appointed full-time city administrators, four have a manager-council form, and two have the commission form of government. For the FY 2005 project, three additional cities plan to participate, one of which (Athens, Tennessee) has a population of less than 25,000.

From its inception, the Tennessee project has collected service and performance data for police, fire, and solid waste collection functions. The definitions of these services have evolved over time to reflect refinements based on measurement experiences and advice from local officials in the participating cities. The service definitions used for the FY 2003 data collection effort, for example, involved the following:

- Police services consist of traditional law enforcement functions, including patrol, investigations, and police administration. The definition encompasses all support personnel and services associated with preventive patrols, traffic enforcement, responding to calls for service, and investigation of crimes, but specifically excludes animal control services and emergency communications (dispatch).
- Fire services include the entire range of services provided by the municipal fire department, which may include fire suppression, fire prevention, fire code inspections, fire safety education, arson investigation, rescue, or emergency medical services.
- Residential refuse collection involves collection of household refuse from residential premises and those small businesses that use residential-sized containers that are collected on the same schedule as residences.

The service definition excludes waste from commercial dumpsters, yard waste and leaves, collection of recyclable materials, and any other special or nonroutine service. Disposal costs (tipping fees) are excluded.[52]

The processes for collecting, reviewing, and cleaning the performance data for participating cities are similar to those employed by the North Carolina project. Organizationally, the Tennessee benchmarking project has a Steering Committee composed mainly of city finance or budget officers and three service committees (police, fire, and solid waste), whose members typically are the department leaders.

The Steering Committee is responsible for reaching agreement on how to define and allocate cost items and for submitting the service profile, cost, and performance data for the fiscal year. Like their counterparts in North Carolina, the Tennessee Steering Committee members make the decisions that shape the policies and practices that comprise the benchmarking effort. Issues that may appear simple at first glance may actually require considerable thought and effort to resolve to all participants' satisfaction. For example, what population figure should be used? Should it be the 2000 census figure, a somewhat more recent population count not yet certified by the state that includes an annexed area, or a current estimate by city officials based on the number of residential utility accounts?

Such issues assume significance especially when a performance measure depends on a per capita ratio. The figure that gets used in the denominator can dramatically affect perceptions of a city's performance. (This is one reason why several benchmarking projects use "per 1,000" population figures in the denominator of such ratios.) Another example of a decision that a steering committee makes is how FTEs are calculated. What data are included in the definition and computation for FTEs affects the values of measures that rely on FTE ratios. For example, should it be based on the total number of hours paid or the budgeted hours? How does this definition affect the unit that has a large volume of overtime charges? Service managers collect and report all service, cost, and performance data to their city's steering committee representative on forms and spreadsheets devised by the MTAS staff.[53]

While resolution of the project's conceptual and methodological issues is critical, equally important is the role that the steering committee has in checking the accuracy of the data that are submitted by their service managers. Benefiting from the North Carolina experience, the Tennessee Steering Committee members meet to review the data submitted by their service managers or chiefs. With draft performance reports from each city in hand, it is possible to identify any outliers or odd results in particular measures. During this data review and cleaning process, the service managers back in the cities are told to be on-call for possible queries that may arise about how they collected, defined, or handled various profile, cost, or performance data. Most detected errors arise from clerical mistakes or misunderstandings about what a particular cost or service item should include or exclude.

While there is continual e-mail communication between MTAS staff and officials in participating cities throughout the year, the schedule for the major activities involved in the Tennessee benchmarking effort for FY 2004–2005 involved the following:

- Data reports due on October 15, 2004 for FY 2004 ending June 30
- Meeting of the Steering Committee in early November 2004 to clean data
- Benchmarking Performance Report published in December 2004
- Steering Committee meeting in early January 2005 to discuss possible changes in definitions, measures, or data collection forms
- Meetings with members of the service committees during spring of 2005 to discuss possible changes or refinements in performance measures
- Meeting of benchmarking participants and other municipal officials in June 2005 to discuss best practices after the meeting of the Tennessee Municipal League

The meeting schedule for the Tennessee project is designed with the aim of producing a final performance report for participants within six months of the close of the fiscal year for which performance data were collected.

Meaningful and valid comparisons of municipal service performance depend on the use of common definitions for each of the cost components for each service relating to personal services, operating expenses, indirect costs, and depreciation. To advance this goal, MTAS staff devised account codes and forms that participating cities use to record the financial data for each municipal service. These financial reporting forms are found in appendix B.

The annual performance report generated by the UT MTAS staff provides a graphic profile of how each city compares on each performance measure with the mean for all cities and the mean for the population group of which it is a part (either above or below 100,000 population). In addition, each city's service delivery system is summarized in narrative profiles. The performance results for police, fire, and solid waste services provided by the smaller cities that participate in the Tennessee project are displayed in tables 5.3, 5.4, and 5.5, respectively.

What conclusions are possible based on a review of these results achieved by cities in the Tennessee project? First, it is clear that all participating cities already have implemented the GASB 34 standards that all communities with annual revenues of less than $10 million were expected to implement beginning

Table 5.3. Police Performance Data for the Smaller Cities in the Tennessee Municipal Benchmarking Program, FY 2003

Inputs Collected	Maryville	Brentwood	Oak Ridge	Collierville	Cleveland	Germantown	Bartlett
population	23,120	26,743	27,337	37,044	37,192	40,203	42,347
city area (sq. mi.)	13	41	92	29	26	20	19.48
road miles	163	423	2 0	257	268	192	261
calls for service	54,218	24,200	32,4 1	34,441	69,610	49,076	42,454
calls dispatched	54,218	24,200	32,4 1	34,441	69,610	49,076	42,454
TIBRS Group A crimes	1424	1006	30 0	1621	3991	1558	2448
TIBRS Group B crimes	249	92	4 5	830	1503	1174	240
number of FTEs	43	53	4	81	91	60	84
number of support	4	3	2	10	11	5	6
traffic accidents	1137	907	16 5	899	2725	885	1186
traffic accidents with injury	171	143	2 3	148	316	104	249
police vehicles	53	61	1	59	117	69	80
maintenance costs	$83,827	$76,575	$283,2 5	$32,423	$355,658	$135,332	$139,517
training costs	$22,921	$57,488	$22,1 6	$45,414	$34,615	$33,357	$37,311
alarm calls	804	3884	25 3	3564	3514	5341	4662
Total cost	$3,278,362	$4,305,193	$3,970,4 5	$5,462,612	$6,127,067	$7,213,177	$7,050,439
Workload							
accidents/road mile	6.98	2.14	8.07	3.50	10.17	4.61	4.54
A&B crimes/1,000 population	72.4	41.1	127.6	66.2	147.7	68.0	63.5
FTEs/1,000 population	1.86	1.98	1.97	2.19	2.45	1.49	1.98
FTEs/road mile	0.26	0.13	0.26	.032	0.34	0.31	.32
FTEs/sq. mile	3.21	1.30	0.59	2.79	3.50	3.03	.08
Efficiency							
cost/1,000 population	$141,798	$160,984	$144,9 5	$147,463	$164,742	$179,419	$166,492
cost/FTEs	$76,241	$81,230	$73,5 7	$67,440	$67,330	$120,220	$83,934
cost/dispatched call	$60	$178	$1 3	$159	$88	$147	$166
incoming calls/FTEs	1,261	457	600	425	765	818	505
dispatched calls/FTEs	1,261	457	600	425	765	818	505
Effectiveness							
traffic injury to accidents ratio	0.15	0.16	0. 3	0.16	0.12	0.12	0.21

Source: Tennessee Municipal Benchmarking Project, *FY 2003 Annual Report* (Knoxville: The University of Tennessee Municipal Technical Advisory Service, 2004).

Table 5.4. Fire Performance Data for the Smaller Cities in the Tennessee Municipal Benchmarking Program, FY 2003

Inputs Collected	Maryville	Brentwood	Oak Ridge	Collierville	Cleveland	Germantown	Bartlett
population	23,120	26,743	27,387	37,044	37,192	40,203	42,347
city area (sq. mi.)	13	41	92	29	26	20	19.48
city road miles	163	423	210	257	268	192	261
nonemergency calls for service	83	356	1432	613	362	28	0
emergency calls for service	1678	1685	1960	1443	331	2110	2773
fire calls	105	95	105	126	271	96	85
structure fires	16	13	44	64	60	45	32
number of FTEs	26	58	49	64	80	68	73
appraised value of properties (mills)	$1741	$1370	≈1600	$2993	$1926	$3964	$2746
EMS service level	1st Resp.	1st Resp.	ALS	ALS	none	ALS	1st Resp.
EMS calls	1047	900	1819	1317	none	1097	2148
ISO rating	3	4	3, 7, 10	4	3	3	3
Total cost	$2,528,271	$4,215,130	$3,5C1,435	$4,984,243	$5,308,507	$5,540,568	$5,449,367
Outputs							
inspections by fire inspectors	737	130	939	1350	342	151	2816
inspections by fire companies	1470	217	1137	459	65	1066	141
fire code violations	960	953	535	1193	561	552	353
fire loss	$419,470	$2,644,840	$5C2,155	$1,133,003	$1,471,425	$806,845	$418,500
Outcomes							
fire service cost/1,000 population	$109,354	$1,57,616	$1⁊,850	$134,549	$142,732	$137,815	$128,684
calls for service/1,000 population	76	76	124	56	19	53	65
fire inspections/1,000 population	95	13	76	49	11	30	70
fire code violations (% cleared)	85%	97%	88%	100%	75%	100%	95%
structure fires/1,000 population	0.7	0.5	1.6	1.7	1.6	1.1	0.8
mean response time	3:31	4:53	4:55	3:34	4:08	4:55	4:50
cost per calls for service	$1,436	$2,065	$1,032	$2,424	$7,660	$2,591	$1,965
fire cause determined	85%	100%	97%	98%	92%	88%	75%

Source: Tennessee Municipal Benchmarking Project, *FY 2003 Annual Report* (Knoxville: The University of Tennessee Municipal Technical Advisory Service, 2004).

Table 5.5. Solid Waste Collection Data for the Smaller Cities in the Tennessee Municipal Benchmarking Program, FY 2003

Inputs Collected	Maryville	Oak Ridge	Collierville	Cleveland	Germantown	Bartlett
population	23,120	27,387	37,044	37,192	40,203	42,347
city area (sq. mi.)	13	92	29	26	20	19.48
city road miles	163	210	257	268	192	261
residential refuse collected (tons)	7,430	11,056	11,900	10,276	13,916	22,800
residential collection points	8,525	11,645	11,200	12,542	11,931	10,074
number of FTEs	6.1		3.7			12.0
service requests	701		397	260	1,041	3,236
collection location:						
curbside	X		X	X		X
back door		X			X	limited
collection frequency:						
once a week	X	X	X	X	X	X
twice a week						
Total cost	$543,348	$951,797	$880,000	$731,986	$3,504,531	$3,130,902
Workload						
tons/1,000 population	321	404	321	276	346	538
tons/1,000 collection points	872	949	1063	819	1166	2263
Efficiency						
cost/ton collected	$73	$86	$74	$71	$252	$137
cost/ton collected curbside	$73		$157	$71		$137
cost/ton collected back door		$86			$252	
cost/collection point	$64	$82	$79	$58	$294	$311
cost/collection point—curbside	$64		$79	$58		$311
cost/collection point—back door	$82	$82			$294	
tons collected/FTE	1,218	n.a.	3182	n.a.	n.a.	1,900
Effectiveness						
service requests/1000 collection points	82	n.a.	35	21	87	321

Source: Tennessee Municipal Benchmarking Project, *FY 2003 Annual Report* (Knoxville: The University of Tennessee Municipal Technical Advisory Service, 2004).

with fiscal years ending after June 15, 2004.[54] The capital asset records and computed deprecation required for the GASB standards facilitate collection of comparable financial data that enable fair comparisons of the cost of providing police, fire, and solid waste collection services in different cities.

It is also apparent in comparing community service profiles that all of the participating cities in the Tennessee benchmarking project are full-service cities that provide a high level of input service quality. Moreover, each participating city must have a chief executive or chief administrative officer who is committed to measuring how well services are performed. These officials must believe that the information collected has some value for helping their local managers to sustain or improve a high level of service performance; otherwise, it is doubtful that they would agree to sustain the effort and resources required to track, gather, and report these performance data.

Like most cities in the other benchmarking projects, the Tennessee communities that participate in the project could be considered artifacts of the "Lake Wobegon" effect in that they may all be above average performers, have little to fear from performance comparisons, and may be among the best-managed and well-run communities in the state anyway.[55] The service profile data for Maryville, Tennessee, indicate, for example, that the city "operates a full-service police department, including school resource officers and community precinct officers . . . the department maintains a 'home fleet' where officers are allowed to drive their police cars home . . . officers work five, eight-hour shifts per week."[56] Although Maryville has no peer in terms of population size and workload that is currently involved in the benchmarking project, its levels of service efficiency and effectiveness for police, fire, and solid waste compare very well with larger participants. In the future, as more cities choose to participate in the benchmarking project, Maryville may well be recognized as one of the highest performing communities among full-service, high-input quality cities with a comparable population and workload profile. As it stands, Maryville can be described as the "best in class" because it is the only one in it among the dozen cities that participated in the FY 2003 project.

Clearly, it makes little sense to attempt to rank-order a dozen participating cities of widely varying size and workload on the same measures of service efficiency or effectiveness and then to claim that city "X" has outperformed city "Y" this year on some particular performance measure. With such a small number of cities, there simply may be too many unique conditions, events, or circumstances, either natural or human-made, that could account for a difference on a performance measure in any one year. In the early stage of a benchmarking project when the number of participating cities is relatively small, it makes more sense to begin to track possible parameters for performance ranges for the different measures for those cities of roughly comparable size, such as those within a ± 5,000 population range. The range parameters for adopted measures can be refined over time as more cities participate and as more years of data suggest a clearer pattern of what constitutes a performance level that is consistently average, above average, or superior for cities with different levels of input service quality (e.g., basic, mid, or high).

LESSONS FROM THE MUNICIPAL BENCHMARKING PROJECTS

Although the municipal benchmarking projects described in this chapter are relatively recent in origin, their experiences suggest a number of lessons that have practical value for officials of smaller communities interested in comparing their city's service performance with other communities and advancing the practice of performance measurement in their communities. The implications of these experiences for future benchmarking efforts are reviewed first, followed by a discussion of the implications for officials in small communities that have an interest in launching or refining a performance measurement effort.

1. Based on our review of contemporary municipal benchmarking projects, the single most important observation is that the linchpin of their success depends on reaching agreement by participants on valid, reliable, and accurate definitions of service, cost, and performance data and ensuring consistent application of these adopted project policies across communities.[57] Each of the benchmarking projects continues to refine its measures and data collection efforts with each passing year. The ICMA Center for Performance Measurement, for example, continues to refine its performance measures, expand the types of services included in its benchmarking project, and attract a growing number of participants. Its training efforts and published resources have significantly advanced the art and science of performance measurement and management during its first decade of operation.

2. Another lesson is that relying on the honor system for consistent interpretation and use of agreed upon service definitions and performance measures is not the most desirable strategy to ensure the accuracy and reliability of the data collected among widely dispersed communities. The benchmarking experiences of North Carolina and Tennessee in particular illustrate the value of having steering committee members gather together to review their own data in light of what other communities have collected or what the computed measures of performance indicate about their city's service. Mistakes, outliers, or nonsensical results can be identified and remedied expeditiously. This data cleaning and integrity process improves the accuracy and utility of the performance measurements for participating communities.

3. Is a benchmarking effort best organized and implemented at a national level or at a state or local level? In one respect, this is an issue about comparing "apples to apples." If performance is going to be compared, local officials want those comparisons to be fair and to be with comparable service operations in peer communities. Local officials tend to be risk-averse, especially since head-to-head performance comparisons have political ramifications. Officials in Fresno, California, for instance, the thirty-seventh largest U.S. city, decided to limit its peer city review to other cities within the state that were close in population size because of the "differing state constitutions and legal authority and financing mechanisms" that affect city operations in other states.[58] They found that cities in different states are more likely to use different fiscal years, have different costs of living, and use different service definitions and accounting procedures, all of which made comparisons with other cities in California much less problematic.[59]

Consequently, the type of benchmarking project that might be more appealing to an audience of small town officials is one that involves other cities in the same state that provide the same type of municipal services. While several factors such as service level, workload, and socioeconomic profile will distinguish communities within a state, they at least share a common state constitutional and statutory environment. Performance comparisons among cities in the same state also have greater promise for mitigating, if not eliminating, some of the data problems related to service and cost comparability.

In addition, there also may be synergistic benefits to having the chief executives, chief financial officers, and service managers from respective cities in a state gather in their respective meetings to discuss, define, share concerns and experiences, and reach agreement on the "what, how, and why" issues associated with measuring and comparing service performance. This is more difficult and certainly more expensive to accomplish among officials who participate in a national project. Face-to-face meetings of municipal officials in a state or regional benchmarking can facilitate arrival at a consensus about how to define a service, how to ascertain its cost, what measures best quantify the outputs and outcomes for each service, and how to present performance information that is truly comparable. In contrast to a packaged program or canned software module, the stakes are higher and more meaningful when local officials have an opportunity to shape the measures applied to their communities.

Meetings among the respective finance officers and service chiefs who participate in state benchmarking projects also provide officials with the opportunity to articulate their stake in the measures that they believe will help their line supervisors and employees to ascertain whether their unit is achieving the level of service efficiency, effectiveness, and quality that they expect it to attain. In other words, it is an opportunity to reflect thoughtfully and share insights about what things should be measured that will "inspire managerial thinking" about how to bring performance in line with expectations.[60] These participating officials consider and reach an understanding about which particular dimensions of a service, such as its speed, accuracy, efficiency, or level of responsiveness, are more or less important in delivering the level of service that they and citizens expect. Sharing opinions about which service dimensions need to be captured by particular performance measures and why they need to be measured helps to stimulate thinking about how the performance results can be used to identify aspects of a service that need improvement.

In the early years of the ICMA project, no standard cost accounting model was employed that distinguished between direct and indirect costs and accounted for other differences in how cities treated other issues such as depreciation of buildings and equipment.[61] Although the ICMA has addressed many of these concerns in recent years, there still may be some municipal officials who question the fairness or comparability of the ICMA cost and performance data.

4. Another lesson that emerges from these benchmarking experiences is that the staff for the project must adeptly navigate the potential minefields endemic to "the politics of comparison." For example, none of the benchmarking projects attempts to rate or rank participants on any single or overall measure of service performance. This practice is prudent. Even if it were possible to conceive of some practical, statistically valid method for doing so, it would be politically unwise from the perspective of local officials and from the standpoint of those interested in advancing community service performance. Why should local officials participate in a benchmarking project that may subject their community to the potential embarrassment of being rated a low or middling service provider? As in state lotteries, there would be few winners and many losers in a performance rating game. The only winners would be those cities that ranked first on a particular service. In such a scenario, one cannot imagine why local officials would expose themselves to the risk of negative publicity by participating in a comparative performance project.

In contrast, the overarching goal of each of the benchmarking projects is to help local officials learn how they might improve service performance, not to heap praise on the top performers or hold up for ridicule the communities that may have lower values on performance measures. Just as a rising tide lifts all boats, a well-designed benchmarking project, founded on mutual trust among participants, can help all participating cities to recognize opportunities and strategies for service improvement. In reality then, local officials have little to fear from explicit performance comparisons.

5. Small cities generally are underrepresented in municipal benchmarking projects. Why don't more small communities participate? Most of the cities

that currently participate in the benchmarking projects are medium or large, full-service, high-input service quality cities. What might attract participation by a larger number of smaller cities in benchmarking projects is a recruitment strategy emphasizing the fairness and utility of performance comparisons. One way to advance such a strategy is to attempt to recruit a larger group of smaller cities with varying levels of input service quality to participate in a benchmarking effort. The labels attached to the three input service quality levels identified in the previous chapter were basic, mid, and high, but other innocuous descriptors could be used, such as good, better, and best.

The objective would be to encourage a broader spectrum of small cities to engage in performance comparisons with the understanding that much could be learned from cohorts with a similar population, workload, and input service quality level. In other words, the outcomes achieved by small cities with more limited service regimes would not be compared to those attained by full-service communities. On the other hand, participants might learn that after accounting for various capital and staff investments, the unit cost for providing a more extensive level of service might not be out of reach financially after all.[62]

6. An enduring concern among municipal officials is whether the cost of participation in a benchmarking project exceeds the benefits. Measuring the performance of municipal services requires a high level of commitment by municipal leaders and a continuing investment by staff in terms of time, effort, and resources. One barrier to more widespread participation in benchmarking efforts may be the up-front costs associated with some programs.

In four of the five existing benchmarking projects, a fee or charge is associated with participation to help defray the project costs, including the support staff who organize meetings, devise reporting forms, process data, and write and publish the annual reports. For example, even though the fees charged by the ICMA are modest when one considers what services are provided, they can seem quite expensive for smaller cities.[63] Likewise, the annual $10,000 fee paid by the participating cities in North Carolina might deter several of the smaller, financially strapped communities in that state. If it were possible to impose modest fees and to subsidize a benchmarking project, at least initially, by a university, state department, or regional association, more small city officials might be induced to participate. The state-level benchmarking efforts, for example, are each managed and sustained by one or two staff members who have this project as one of their job responsibilities.

7. Perhaps the issue that represents the greatest remaining challenge for contemporary benchmarking efforts is the difficulties inherent in connecting or attributing high performance levels by some cities with particular policies, practices, attributes, or assets that other cities might be able to adapt and implement to achieve similar performance success. Unlike most private sector

production activities, it is much more difficult to attribute some performance outcome to one or even a few particular practices, policies, innovations, or ideas. It is probably much more likely that "better" practices rather than "best" practices can be identified among participating communities. As noted previously, benchmarking is very unlikely to reveal a bundle of specific actions that will magically produce spectacular service improvements. If benchmarking is a catalyst for a performance improvement, the chances are that some other strategy may get the credit for it.[64] Ammons aptly illustrates that if a community discovers deficiencies in a department's performance and decides to contract out the service, privatization may get the credit for a performance gain.[65]

Much of what local government does involves labor intensive services. The people a city employs can and do make a substantial difference in how well services are performed. So, the first and most logical source for potential explanations of performance differences are the professional training, experience, knowledge, and abilities of the people who supervise and provide the services. In this respect, it is noteworthy that most of the cities that participate in contemporary benchmarking projects enjoy the services of a full-time city manager or city administrator. This suggests that the level of professionalism among municipal executives makes a difference at least with respect to the recognized value of measuring and seeking ways to improve services through benchmarking.

While there is no explicit linkage between best practices and results achieved using the same performance measures, the annual "bright ideas" award competition conducted by the Northwest Municipal Conference is an effective strategy for rapidly sharing ideas and practices that some communities have found to improve service quality. In North Carolina and Tennessee, the common strategy for connecting performance outcomes and ideas for performance improvement is to facilitate networking among municipal officials in an annual meeting that involves discussions among benchmarking participants and presentations by local officials who have achieved desirable performance results.

These are perfectly appropriate "low-tech" but potentially highly productive opportunities to exchange information and insights. Eventually, as more communities participate in formal benchmarking projects, it will be possible for project staff to collect more detailed information on a broader array of specific community features, staff profiles, service policies, and service processes that will permit more reliable statistical analysis of the factors that may help to explain performance differences among communities. At the very least, such analyses can help to distinguish the factors that affect performance that are within and outside the control of municipal officials.

IMPLICATIONS OF BENCHMARKING PROJECTS FOR SMALL COMMUNITIES

What can small town officials interested in performance measurement and management learn from these benchmarking projects? In the first place, measuring performance is a lot like keeping score in a ball game; it is hard to know who is ahead or behind unless someone keeps score. For small city officials (as well as others) who wish to understand how well their service operations perform, that performance has to be measured in ways that matter to the community.

Where should small city officials begin? Before selecting measures, it is necessary to establish the mission and goals for local services and programs. These embrace what things a service is supposed to do or accomplish that are important to the community. Once these goals are articulated, only then does it make sense to gather the types of information that can help local officials to determine whether service goals are being achieved.

However, just gathering a slew of performance statistics on the important dimensions of a service does not automatically produce the kind of information helpful for making decisions about service improvement. Most performance measures require the collection of other data on community characteristics and service resources so that information can be generated that is useful for making management decisions. For example, "setout rate," an effectiveness measure for residential recycling service, would require information on the total number of residential collection points serviced as a percentage of those households that are eligible to receive collection of household recyclables. This measure also would require decisions about what actually constitutes a "setout": any material in any amount on any collection day, or a more circumspect measure that might count only those households that bring recyclables to the curb at least twice in a four-week period? Setout rates might also be computed for different types of materials. Knowing the values for a setout measure can help service managers to ascertain who recycles what and with what frequency. With this information, local officials might be able to target education efforts, consider the impacts of changes in service frequency and schedule, or take other action to increase the level of participation in recycling.

The measures selected by the benchmarking participants shown in appendix A provide a useful starting point for local discussions about what types of measures might be most appropriate and useful. As noted in the introduction to this chapter, there is no boilerplate set of best performance measures; local service goals and objectives vary too much. However, the performance measures employed by benchmarking participants have survived a rigorous crucible of review and refinement over several years by local service chiefs. Consequently, these measures are worth considering by other communities.

To help narrow the range of choices somewhat, consultations with staff in the benchmarking projects yielded several suggestions for measures that participating communities considered to be particularly useful indicators of the different aspects of their service delivery and performance. In police services, for example, chiefs are particularly keen on measuring staffing levels, including sworn officers and FTEs, as service inputs because of the significance these indicators have in terms of patrol availability and ability to respond swiftly to service calls. Among the measures of police service efficiency, crimes cleared by type per sworn officer touch on both investigation and apprehension dimensions of police work. For measuring the effectiveness of traffic enforcement efforts, the traffic injuries to accidents ratio has strong support among police chiefs in Tennessee.[66] Cities in the South Carolina project place considerable value on police response times and the results from citizen surveys, especially the proportions that rate the service good or excellent.[67] Several resources are available for how to use indicators of police workload and performance judiciously.[68]

For both police and fire/paramedic services, an important measure of effoo tiveness is the total time between a service call and arrival on the scene. The speed of response times affect citizen perceptions about the quality of service and the prospects of suspect apprehension or the extent of fire losses sustained. Firefighting professionals also have a keen interest in the training level of their staff. Staff who are trained in a wide range of skills that include inspections, firefighting, emergency medical services, hazardous materials handling, testing hydrants, and arson investigation are not only busier but also enable the city to provide a higher level of input service quality. The normally substantial downtime for firefighters can be filled with other activities if staff are qualified to perform them. Staff training levels comprise part of the ISO's fire suppression rating schedule. To track some of these other activities, several projects employ efficiency measures of the number of inspections completed per inspector FTE or per 1,000 population. The effectiveness of fire suppression, for example, is measured by the percentage of fires confined to the room of origin. The effectiveness of fire investigations is measured in two benchmarking projects by the percent of fires for which a cause is determined.

The data collection effort associated with evaluating the performance of solid waste services involves relatively few variables. Once service profile and input data on staff, equipment, and the service population are collected, the main variables of interest in efficiency measures are costs and volume, and the main variables in effectiveness are complaints and service requests. Cost per ton collected or cost per collection point are commonly used measures of efficiency. Complaints or service requests per 1,000 collection points are employed by communities in both North Carolina and Tennessee. The percentage of the waste stream reduced through recycling is a measure of the effectiveness used by North Carolina.

When it comes to the actual use of performance data, its most immediate value lies in its diagnostic potential. With performance results in hand, local officials can determine whether a service performance gap exists between a goal and actual service performance. With multiple years of performance data, trends in service performance can be identified. The North Carolina project, for example, facilitates trend analysis by presenting graphs that show how current year performance compares to the performance achieved on each measure during the two previous years.

Measuring performance is not an end in itself. What spans the gulf between performance measurement and performance management is the actual use of performance results to identify the service dimensions that need improvement. Small city officials could benefit by participating in a benchmarking project that involves performance comparisons. While benchmarking is only one means to an end, it offers significant potential for bridging the gap between existing performance and performance aspirations. Ideas and strategies for service improvement are more likely to be identified if a community participates with peers that employ the same performance measures, network on a regular basis, and share a commitment to service improvement.

SUMMARY

For small city officials interested in measuring and improving the performance of local services, it is worthwhile to review what has been learned about performance measurement based on the experiences of the cities engaged in contemporary municipal benchmarking projects. Among the benefits of such a review are being able to distinguish the different types of measures and what they indicate about services, narrowing the range of performance measures that have potential local applicability by considering those that have been refined over time by groups of municipal service chiefs across the country, and understanding the importance of data verification and accuracy. In addition, small town officials need not fear what performance measures or what performance comparisons might show. The potential benefits of learning what practices and policies promote sustained high performance among cities with comparable levels of input service quality far outweigh, in our judgment, the costs associated with measuring performance or any perceived political risks of doing so. At the very least, if local officials believe their communities are doing the right things, using appropriate performance measures will likely result in getting more of whatever is being measured for any service. Doing the right things as well as possible is the promise offered by measuring performance and actually using this information to improve services. Participation in a municipal benchmarking project can help small communities to identify and adapt ideas that have the potential to enhance service performance.

NOTES

1. Joseph S. Wholey and Harry P. Hatry, "The Case for Performance Monitoring," *Public Administration Review* 52, no. 6 (1992): 604–10; The Governmental Accounting and Standards Board (GASB) views performance measurement as a form of non-financial accountability necessary for assessing accountability and making informed decisions about the economy, efficiency, and effectiveness of the services provided. See www.seagov.org/sea_gasb_project/con_stmt_two.shtml (accessed October 22, 2004) For GASB recommendations about how to report and communicate performance information effectively, see the 2003 GASB report *Reporting Performance Information: Suggested Criteria for Effective Communication* at www.seagov.org/ sea_gasb_project/suggested_criteria_report.pdf (accessed October 22, 2004).

2. Robert S. Kaplan and David P. Norton, "The Balanced Scorecard: Measures That Drive Performance," *Harvard Business Review* (January–February 1992): 71–79.

3. See, for example, ICMA, *Performance Management: When Results Matter,* 2004, at www2.icma.org/upload/bc/attach/%7BEDFADAF9–80BB-4BF4-A7EE-4D86A2812527%7DPerfMeas_small.pdf (accessed September 2, 2004); Joseph S. Wholey, "Performance-Based Management: Responding to the Challenge," *Public Productivity and Management Review* 22, no. 3 (1999): 288–307; Patria de Lancer Julnes and Marc Holzer, "Promoting the Utilization of Performance Measures in Public Organizations: An Empirical Study of Factors Affecting Adoption and Implementation," *Public Administration Review* 61, no. 6 (2001): 693–708; Mary Kopczynski and Michael Lombardo, "Comparative Performance Measurement: Insights and Lessons Learned from a Consortium Effort," *Public Administration Review* 59, no. 2 (1999): 124–34; Frank P. Williams, Marilyn D. McShane, and Dale Sechrest, "Barriers to Effective Performance Review," *Public Administration Review* 54, no. 6 (1994): 537–42. For insight into the history and concept of managing for results see Jonathan Walters, Mark Abrahams, and James Fountain, "Managing for Results—An Overview," in *Reporting Performance Information: Suggested Criteria for Effective Communication* (Governmental Accounting and Standards Board, 2003), at www.seagov .org/aboutpmg/mfr_chap3.pdf (accessed October 22, 2004).

4. The best single resource for information on performance measures appropriate for the various dimensions of a variety of services is David N. Ammons, *Municipal Benchmarks: Performance and Establishing Community Standards* (Thousand Oaks, Calif.: Sage, 2001); see also the resources on performance measurement available

from the ICMA at www2.icma.org/main/topic.asp?tpid=18&hsid=1 (accessed October 22, 2004); see also reports from the National Civic League at www.ncl.org.

5. William C. Rivenbark and Janet M. Kelly, "Management Innovation in Smaller Municipal Government," *State and Local Government Review* 35, no. 3 (2003): 196–205.

6. Harry P. Hatry, *Performance Measurement* (Washington, D.C.: The Urban Institute Press, 1999); and Ammons, *Municipal Benchmarks*.

7. Theodore H. Poister and Gregory Streib, "Performance Measurement in Municipal Government: Assessing the State of the Practice," *Public Administration Review* 59, no. 4 (1999): 325–35.

8. David N. Ammons, Charles Coe, and Michael Lombardo, "Performance Comparison Projects in Local Government: Participants' Perspectives," *Public Administration Review* 61, no. 1 (2001): 100–110; and David H. Folz, "Service Quality and Benchmarking the Performance of Municipal Services," *Public Administration Review*, 64, no. 2 (2004): 209–20.

9. Walters et al., "Managing for Results."

10. Steven Cohen and William Eimicke, *Tools for Innovators: Creative Strategies for Managing Public Sector Organizations* (San Francisco: Jossey-Bass, 1998); Patricia Keehley et al., *Benchmarking for Best Practices in the Public Sector: Achieving Performance Breakthroughs in Federal, State, and Local Agencies* (San Francisco: Jossey-Bass, 1997); Charles Coe, "Local Government Benchmarking: Lessons from Two Major Efforts," *Public Administration Review* 59, no. 2 (1999): 110–23.

11. David N. Ammons, "A Proper Mentality for Benchmarking," *Public Administration Review* 59, no. 2 (1999): 105–9.

12. David N. Ammons, "Performance Measurement and Managerial Thinking," *Public Performance and Management Review* 25, no. 4 (2002): 344–47. Ammons explained that managers should be prepared to persuade skeptics, especially at the operational level, that the benefits of performance measurement will outweigh the costs associated with gathering and analyzing performance data. The performance measures chosen should "tap service dimensions that the unit's members want to be known for" and enable supervisors "to gauge their progress toward earning that reputation."

13. Janet M. Kelly and William C. Rivenbark, *Performance Budgeting for State and Local Government* (Armonk, N.Y.: M. E. Sharpe, 2003); and Ammons, *Municipal Benchmarks*.

14. Kelly and Rivenbark, *Performance Budgeting for State and Local Government*.

15. Ammons, *Municipal Benchmarks*.

16. Ammons, *Municipal Benchmarks*.

17. Folz, "Service Quality and Benchmarking," 209–20.

18. Keehley et al., *Benchmarking for Best Practices*.

19. Keehley et al., *Benchmarking for Best Practices*; Cohen and Eimicke, *Tools for Innovators*.

20. Ammons et al., "Performance-Comparison Projects"; Ammons, "A Proper Mentality."

21. Coe, "Local Government Benchmarking."

22. International City/County Management Association Center for Performance Measurement, *Comparative Performance Measurement FY2002 Data Report* (Washington, D.C.: ICMA Press, 2003).

23. Kelly and Rivenbark, *Performance Budgeting for State and Local Government.*

24. Rex Barton, police consultant, University of Tennessee Municipal Technical Advisory Service, personal communication with author, October 18, 2004.

25. Ammons, *Municipal Benchmarks.*

26. ICMA, *Comparative Performance Measurement;* see also the information at the links found at www2.icma.org/ (accessed October 22, 2004).

27. ICMA, *Comparative Performance Measurement.*

28. International City/County Management Association, *What Is the Fee to Participate in the Performance Measurement Program?*, n.d., at www2.icma.org/main/bc .asp?bcid=108&hsid=1&ssid1=50&ssid2=220&ssid3=302#2 (accessed November 4, 2004).

29. ICMA, *Comparative Performance Measurement*, 137.

30. ICMA, *Comparative Performance Measurement*, 513.

31. ICMA, at www2.icma.org/main/bc.asp?bcid=108&hsid=1&ssid1=50&ssid2= 220&ssid3=302.

32. Coe, "Local Government Benchmarking."

33. Northwest Municipal Conference, *How Do Government Organizations Evaluate Their Performance?*, n.d., at www.citytechusa.com/pdf/eMeasure.pdf (accessed November 4, 2004). There is a modest $100 fee for the base module in the Dynamic Government Performance Measurement program and an additional $100 fee for each service module that a city chooses to use.

34. Liangfu Wu and Larry Bruce, *Introduction of Dynamic Government Performance Measurement* (Chicago: Northwest Municipal Conference and CityTech USA, 2004); also Shalen Hunter, program associate, Northwest Municipal Conference, personal communication with author, October 4, 2004.

35. Northwest Municipal Conference, *Bright Ideas: A Project of the NWMC Best Practices Committee* (Chicago: Northwest Municipal Conference, 2004).

36. Northwest Municipal Conference, *2002–2003 Best Practices Awards,* 2004, at www.nwmc-cog.org/jahia/Jahia/pid/43 (accessed November 4, 2004).

37. Northwest Municipal Conference, *Bright Ideas.*

38. North Carolina Local Government Performance Measurement Project, *FY 2002–2003 Performance and Cost Data Report* (Chapel Hill: University of North Carolina Institute of Government, February 2004); Kelly and Rivenbark, *Performance Budgeting for State and Local Government*; and David N. Ammons and William C. Rivenbark, " Benchmarking and Performance Measurement" (seminar, University of Tennessee Municipal Technical Advisory Service Conference, Cookeville, Tennessee, April 21, 2004).

39. Kelly and Rivenbark, *Performance Budgeting for State and Local Government.*

40. Kelly and Rivenbark, *Performance Budgeting for State and Local Government.*

41. North Carolina Local Government Performance Measurement Project, *FY 2002–2003 Performance and Cost Data Report.*

42. North Carolina Local Government Performance Measurement Project, *FY 2002–2003 Performance and Cost Data Report*, 9.

43. Ammons and Rivenbark, "Benchmarking and Performance Measurement."

44. Institute for Public Service and Policy Research, *South Carolina Municipal Benchmarking Project FY 2001 Annual Report* (Columbia: University of South Carolina, 2002).

45. Institute for Public Service and Policy Research, *South Carolina Municipal Benchmarking Project.* Additional information on the definition of performance measures used for the four services included in the project is available at www.iopa.sc.edu/grs/scmbp/SCMBP_services.asp (accessed November 4, 2004). The University of South Carolina's Institute for Public Service and Policy Research's Governmental Research and Services unit charges a modest fee for participation in the benchmarking project that ranges from $1,000 to $3,000 depending on city size, ability to pay, and the number of services the city chooses to include in the benchmarking effort.

46. Institute for Public Service and Policy Research, *South Carolina Municipal Benchmarking Project.* The citizen surveys that gather information on service quality measures are conducted biennially.

47. Anna Berger, project director, University of South Carolina Institute for Public Service and Policy Research, personal communication with author, October 4, 2004.

48. Institute for Public Service and Policy Research, *South Carolina Municipal Benchmarking Project.*

49. Institute for Public Service and Policy Research, *South Carolina Municipal Benchmarking Project.*

50. Institute for Public Service and Policy Research, *South Carolina Municipal Benchmarking Project.*

51. Institute for Public Service and Policy Research, *South Carolina Municipal Benchmarking Project.*

52. Alan Major, *Tennessee Municipal Benchmarking Project, FY 2003 Annual Report* (Knoxville: University of Tennessee Municipal Technical Advisory Service, 2004).

53. MTAS staff: Alan Major, finance and accounting consultant, University of Tennessee Municipal Technical Advisory Service, is the primary staff person for the Tennessee Benchmarking project. Ron Darden, consultant, University of Tennessee Municipal Technical Advisory Service.

54. The major innovations of Statement 34 required governments to report on the *overall* state of the government's financial health, not just its individual funds; to provide more complete information about the cost of delivering services to their citizens; and to include for the first time information about the government's public infrastructure assets such as bridges, roads, and storm sewers. Among the chief objectives of GASB 34 was to encourage the use of full accrual accounting for all government activities including not just current assets and liabilities (such as cash and accounts payable) but also capital assets and long-term liabilities (such as infrastructure and general obligation debt). The idea is to enhance accountability by making the financial condition of the city and the full cost of providing services more apparent and transparent and to encourage the use of performance measures that indicate how effectively

the local government uses resources to provide programs and services. For more information see accounting.rutgers.edu/raw/gasb/repmodel/oview34.pdf (accessed November 10, 2004).

55. Ammons, *Municipal Benchmarks.*

56. Major, *Tennessee Municipal Benchmarking Project.*

57. Kelly and Rivenbark, *Performance Budgeting for State and Local Government.*

58. Daniel Hobbs, "How to Benchmark with Easily Available Resources: Ensure That You're Comparing Apples to Apples," *Public Management* 86, no. 8 (2004): 16.

59. Coe, "Local Government Benchmarking."

60. Ammons, "Performance Measurement and Managerial Thinking."

61. Coe, "Local Government Benchmarking."

62. Ray Crouch, fire consultant, University of Tennessee Municipal Technical Advisory Service, personal communication with author, October 14, 2004.

63. ICMA charges a one-time training fee of $3,900; an annual participation fee of $5,000; and a $7,500 fee for any community that chooses to participate in the National Citizen Survey, a mail survey sent to a random sample of 1,200 households in the locality. See Hobbs, "How to Benchmark with Easily Available Resources.

64. Ammons, "Performance Measurement and Managerial Thinking."

65. Ammons, "Performance Measurement and Managerial Thinking."

66. Rex Barton, police consultant, University of Tennessee Municipal Technical Advisory Service), personal communication with author, October 18, 2004; and Al Major, finance and accounting consultant, University of Tennessee Municipal Technical Advisory Service, personal communication with author November 16, 2004.

67. Anna Berger, Institute for Public Service and Policy Research, University of South Carolina, e-mail to author, November 24, 2004.

68. See, for example Charles K. Coe and Deborah Lamm Wiesel, "Police Budgeting: Winning Strategies," *Public Administration Review* 61, no. 6 (2001): 718–27; Ammons, *Municipal Benchmarks*; Harry P. Hatry, Louis H. Blair, Donald M. Fisk, John M. Greiner, John R. Hall, and Phillip S. Schaeman, *How Effective Are Your Community Services?* (Washington, D.C.: American Enterprise Institute, 1992).

6

Conclusion

In this concluding chapter it is appropriate to confess that we have a certain measure of fondness for small communities and an abiding appreciation for the efforts of their public servants who labor, often under very challenging circumstances, to make a positive difference in people's lives and in the quality of community life. The genesis for this perspective is rooted in our public service experiences with small communities prior to entering academia. This view became fully formed only after some reflection about how much we had learned about the art and craft of public administration from the extraordinarily talented managers and mayors with whom we had the good fortune to work. These experiences cemented our conviction that the abilities and skills of individuals who hold positions of administrative responsibility can and do make a significant difference in small communities. That difference always seemed to be most apparent in the extent to which citizens are helped, needs are addressed, services are efficient, and rights are protected.

One of the motivations for pursuing this research project was to investigate whether empirical evidence confirmed or contradicted this conviction as it applied to executive involvement in the governmental process, the executive decision-making process, and the level of services provided. Happily, evidence confirmed that important differences did exist in these respects. The profile of participants in benchmarking projects also suggested that the prospects for measuring performance and using this information to help improve services might be greater in professionally managed small communities.

The value added to the governance and management of small communities by having the services of a professional city manager or administrator was the recurring theme of this book. This chapter reviews the ways in which professionalism mattered and highlights other findings about small communities.

The reader now has a clearer picture of the demographic trends, governmental features, chief executive characteristics, and issues that figure prominently on the agendas of small communities. While stereotypes fade slowly from the national consciousness, the image of small communities as places of stagnation or decline is exceptionally inaccurate. During the 1990s, most small communities experienced population growth rather than decline. The mean growth rate for small cities exceeded the national growth rate during that decade. By 2000, most small communities were designated as being located within one of the Census Bureau's urban areas, with many on the fringe of or engulfed by exurban growth. Small communities still tend to be more socially homogeneous than larger cities, but in terms of income and educational profiles of their residents, they are more alike than different from other Americans.

The changes in governmental structure experienced among larger cities also have swept through the town halls of America's small communities. While a slim majority of small cities retained a mayor-council charter form on paper, many small cities adopted features of the council-manager form. By 1999, most small cities had a governmental structure best described as "adaptive." Adaptive communities are likely to have a full-time CAO, a directly elected mayor with veto powers, and council members elected from a mix of district and at-large races. It was apparent that an increasing number of officials in small communities recognized the value of having the services of a full-time professional administrator, perhaps in response to pressures for enhanced service efficiency and accountability for service performance. In addition, we found that although communities with city managers tended to have larger populations than cities with mayoral chief executives, the mean size of their municipal workforces was actually smaller when measured on a per capita basis.

Several characteristics distinguished mayors and city managers, most notable of which were differences in their level and type of education, their political partisanship, and their career path to the chief executive's office. While the vast majority of mayors attained a bachelor's degree, most frequently in business, more than 60 percent of city managers had at least a master's degree. Almost two-thirds of city managers received master's degrees in public administration.

That this professional training may have inculcated a sensitivity to the value of politically neutral competence in administration is evidenced by the large proportion of city managers who expressed no political party preference. By contrast, most mayors expressed a party preference, with about equal proportions supporting each of the two major parties.

Mayors and city managers in small communities also had distinct career paths. For the largest proportion of mayors, the most common springboard to higher elected office was service on the local legislative body. For city managers, previous experience as city manager in another city or as assistant city manager in the same or a different city were the most commonly held positions prior to their current one. Stability in the office of chief executive appeared to be the norm for both mayors and city managers in small cities; the average tenure for each was about seven years.

Among all chief executives, there was general agreement about the most significant issues that confronted their communities. Most prominent on local agendas were problems related to a deteriorating transportation infrastructure. For many executives, concern about the adequacy and safety of the local transportation system may have been elevated, at least in part, by the higher traffic volumes that accompanied their city's population growth. Another significant problem on which consensus emerged was local economic development. Attracting new private investments not only helps to create more local job opportunities, but it also remains the most popular way for local officials to obtain additional tax resources to address pressing infrastructure and service needs. An eminently feasible future research project, for example, would be to analyze whether professionally managed small communities are more successful than their counterparts in attracting new economic development.

Interesting differences emerged among mayors and city managers in terms of how they allocated their time among activities related to their policy and management roles and how extensively they were involved in each of the four dimensions of the governmental process. Since about two-thirds of mayors are part-time, they would be expected to allocate their time somewhat differently than full-time city managers. As a group, mayors allocated significantly less time to their management role than do city managers. However, there was no significant difference among mayors and city managers in terms of the amount of time they allocated to their policy role. In fact, the amount of time that mayors who have a CAO spent on their policy role was virtually identical to the time that city managers allocated to it. This finding suggests that mayors and city managers place about equal value or weight on the importance of proposing and developing policy to address community needs. It certainly belies the notion that unelected city managers are bent on dominating or controlling local policy making, at least in terms of how they allocate their time.

However, when it comes to the extent of involvement that chief executives have in the dimensions of the governmental process, city managers exhibited a statistically higher level of involvement than mayors with or without a CAO. This suggests that the overall size of the "time or effort pies" for mayors and city managers was quite different. It is one thing to find that both mayors and city managers allocate about the same proportion of their time to their policy and management roles. It is quite another to learn that the magnitude of engagement by city managers in specific activities related to mission, policy, administration, and management is qualititatively different.

That city managers in administrative government structures have a more extensive level of involvement and engagement in decisions related to the various dimensions of the governmental process does not imply that they operate outside of local political control. Rather, it raises a more compelling question about who is attending to policy and administrative issues in cities that lack a professional city manager. In this respect, the value added to communities with city managers consisted of having a chief executive who was more deeply and extensively engaged in and, consequently, more overtly accountable for the decisions made in each of the dimensions of the governmental process. By contrast, a less extensively engaged elected chief executive may be more likely, as Charles Goodsell reminds us, to blame others in the city bureaucracy for policy failures or service problems.[1] In a professional city management regime, virtually everyone knows where the buck stops.

Our own experiences in small city management taught us that city managers usually operate differently from mayors, especially with respect to the process they employ to reach decisions about service policies and issues. We speculated that a difference in the pattern of decision making among executives might help to explain why city managers indicated a more extensive level of engagement in decisions related to the governmental process. In fact, city managers were found to exhibit a consistently more extensive pattern of consultation with key groups of community stakeholders in the process of making decisions about a number of local services and programs. City managers consulted much more frequently with members of the city council and with department heads in reaching decisions. A more extensive pattern of consultation requires more effort and time from an executive. Consequently, it makes eminent sense for city managers to exhibit a more extensive level of involvement in the governmental process.

An asset historically attributed to elected chief executives has been that they are more likely to be responsive to various community interests since their office is attained through the choices made in the election booth. However, no statistically significant difference was found among mayors and city managers in the extent to which they perceived their decisions to be subject to influence by community interests linked to a number of different services. Both types of executives perceived that community interests had minor to moderate influence on their decisions.

Professional administrators add value to the small community in another important respect. Controlling for differences in size, metropolitan status, and wealth, the communities that have city managers and administrative structures tended to provide a qualitatively higher level of service based on a cumulative score of service quality for police, fire, building inspections, and solid waste recycling services. Having a city manager or an administrative structure was found to be particularly important for the small communities with populations over 15,000, regardless of whether their median household incomes were below or above the norm. This finding suggests that as small communities become the residence of choice for more citizens, professional city managers can be expected to advocate and work to develop a higher level of service quality to meet the perceived needs of a growing urban center. We speculate that the observed higher service quality level among administrative cities in particular may be additional evidence of city managers' responsiveness to community service needs.

There is widespread agreement among both scholars and practitioners that service quality is important. However, there have been few efforts in the public administration field to specify exactly what it is, how to measure it, and how to use this information to help improve services. To help fill this void and to suggest fruitful avenues for future research, the importance of the input and output dimensions of service quality were explained and indicators for the dimensions of output service quality were suggested. A conceptual model of service quality suggested factors that affect citizen and client perceptions of output service quality and consequent levels of satisfaction with service performance. This model also has some diagnostic potential for identifying the points or gaps in the service process that might be among the reasons why citizen perceptions of service quality and performance are less than desired.

Applying available proxy indicators of input service quality to four services provided by most small communities demonstrated the feasibility of measuring input service quality. Substantial variation in input service quality was found to occur among small communities. Almost one-fifth provided services at a high quality level, about 47 percent provided a middle range of quality, and about one-third provided a basic service level.

Accounting for differences in the level of input service quality among communities was shown to have particular value for enhancing the utility, value, and fairness of performance comparisons. We speculated that high performing service operations may exist in each level of input service quality and that more small community officials might be encouraged to use performance measures and to participate in performance comparisons if they could learn what other cities with a comparable service level and workload do to attain higher performance levels.

While relatively few small communities measure the performance of their services, we found some evidence to suggest city managers and CAOs are probably more likely to have an interest in doing so, particularly if participation by their counterparts in larger cities is any indication. To help advance interest in and understanding of performance measurement, we discussed the different types of measures, their relationship to the different elements of service and program logic, and the different approaches to performance benchmarking. The experiences of contemporary municipal benchmarking efforts were reviewed with the aim of extracting findings of interest to the staff for benchmarking projects and highlighting the implications for municipal officials who wish to measure performance and use this information to improve services.

Officials in small communities now have a resource that compiles the measures of service output, efficiency, and effectiveness that have been refined over several years of experience and received intensive scrutiny by municipal service chiefs and financial officers. Although the diversity of community service goals and objectives obviates any ideal set of performance measures appropriate for all cities, this menu is a good place to begin a measure selection process.

The best prospects for linking performance outcomes to actions that may improve services is participation in a benchmarking project. Providing that more state and regional organizations persuade and engage their respective cities in benchmarking efforts that compare performance outcomes among communities with comparable service quality and workloads, the future may auger significant advances in municipal service performance.

If professional training in the art and craft of public administration is to have broader appeal outside the boundaries of professional organizations and the halls of academia, the value added by professional local government administration must be documented and measured in its multiple possible manifestations. This research has documented several of the ways that professionalism makes an important difference, particularly with respect to executive behavior and the level of service quality provided in a community.

DIRECTIONS FOR FUTURE RESEARCH

Future research should pursue several avenues of inquiry about the value added by professional city administrators. For example, to what extent may small communities with professional managers experience more success in attracting and retaining economic investment? Are professionally managed communities more likely to measure and actually use performance measures and management systems? Public administration scholars also should seek to refine measures of service quality using community-specific data on service budgets, staff qualifications, staff levels and experience, available equipment and technology, and types of facilities. Finally, the responsibility for launching additional benchmarking projects rests with university, state, and regional organizations. These units need contribute only a few well-trained staff resources to support these efforts. Among the dividends such projects can yield if they include an array of communities with varying size and workload is the potential to determine whether professional management is responsible for higher levels of service performance, particularly among smaller communities.

The story of those who govern and manage small communities continues to unfold. It is a story that demands to be told. This work represents only an initial volume in that saga, one that hopefully will inspire subsequent scholarly inquiries into governance and management issues among small communities. Public service careers in small communities offer amazing opportunities coupled with tremendous responsibilities. Individual professionals can and do make a significant difference in these communities. For those interested in a professional city management career, it is hoped that this book helps to deepen interest in and knowledge about the challenging and rewarding world of small city management.

NOTES

1. Charles T. Goodsell, *The Case for Bureaucracy: A Public Administration Polemic* (Washington, D.C.: CQ Press, 2003).

Appendix A

MEASURES USED FOR POLICE, FIRE, SOLID WASTE, AND RECYCLING SERVICES IN MUNICIPAL BENCHMARKING PROJECTS

Measures for Police Services	North Carolina	Tennessee	South Carolina	ICMA*
Inputs				
Alarm calls		•		
Average length of service for sworn officers	•			
Calls actually dispatched		•		
Calls for police patrol services divided by police per 1,000 service population			•	
Calls for service		•		
City area square miles		•		
City road miles		•		
City unemployment rate			•	
County unemployment rate			•	
Daytime population				•
Dollars earmarked for victims/witness advocacy program			•	
Form of government				•
Jail and holding-facility characteristics				•
Maintenance costs		•		

Inputs—Police Services (continued)	North Carolina	Tennessee	South Carolina	ICMA
Median family income (county)	•		•	
Median household income				•
Number of Full Time Equivalents (FTEs)		•		
Number of investigators divided by police per 1,000 service area population			•	
Number of police patrol officers			•	
Number of support personnel		•		
Number of sworn officers	•			
Part I crimes—persons	•		•	
Part I crimes—property	•		•	
Part I crimes total	•		•	
Percentage below poverty level				•
Percentage of juveniles				•
Percentage owner-occupied housing				•
Percentage unemployed (unemployed rate)	•			•
Police department accreditation status	•			
Police vehicles		•		
Population		•		•
Population density				•
Population inside city limits			•	
Population outside city limits			•	
Reporting format UCR versus IBR	•			
Residential population served				•
Service area inside city limits			•	
Service area outside city limits			•	
Service area population			•	
Service area total square miles			•	
Size of service area compared with size of town, city, or county				•
Specialized features of police services				•
Square miles				•
State three strikes law status				•

Inputs—Police Services (continued)	North Carolina	Tennessee	South Carolina	ICMA
TIBRS group A crimes		•		
TIBRS group B crimes		•		
Total budgeted FTEs				•
Total cost for all police services		•	•	
Total general fund operating expense (millions)				•
Total number of 911 incoming calls			•	
Total number of accident reports			•	
Total number of assaults to officers divided by police per 1,000 service area population			•	
Total number of incident reports			•	
Total sworn full-time employees divided by police per 1,000 service area population			•	
Traffic accidents	•	•		
Traffic accidents with injury		•		
Training costs		•		
Outputs/Workload—Police Services				
Number of top priority police calls per 1,000 population				•
Calls dispatched per 1,000 population	•			
Calls for police patrol services divided by police per 1,000 service area population			•	
TIBRS group A and B crimes per 1,000 population		•		
UCR part I crimes per 1,000 population	•			•
Total arrest for UCR part I crimes per 1,000 population				•
Total arrests for UCR part I (violent) crimes per 1,000 population				•
Total arrests for UCR part I (property) crimes per 1,000 population				•
UCR part I crimes against persons—reported per 1,000 population				•

Outputs/Workload— *Police Services (continued)*	*North Carolina*	*Tennessee*	*South Carolina*	*ICMA*
UCR part I crimes against property— reported per 1,000 population				•
Total UCR part I crimes reported divided by police—per 1,000 service area population			•	
UCR part I crimes against persons divided by police—per 1,000 service area population			•	
UCR part I crimes against property divided by police—per 1,000 service area population			•	
Percent of UCR part I crimes against persons—cleared			•	•
Percent of UCR part I crimes against property—cleared			•	•
Percentage of UCR part I crimes (violent) assigned to investigators				•
Percentage of UCR part I crimes (property) assigned to investigators				•
Total arrests for UCR part II drug offenses per 1,000 population				•
Total arrests for UCR part I crimes per sworn full time equivalent				•
Juvenile arrests for UCR part I crimes (violent) as a percentage of total arrests for UCR part I crimes				•
Juvenile arrests for UCR part I crimes (property) as a percentage of total arrests for UCR part I crimes				•
Total arrests per 1,000 population				•
Juvenile arrests for part II drug abuse offenses as a percentage of total arrests for UCR part II drug offenses				•
DUI arrests per 1,000 population				•
Traffic violations per 1,000 population			•	
Traffic accidents per road mile		•		
Number of fatal traffic accidents per 1,000 population				•

Outputs/Workload— Police Services (continued)	North Carolina	Tennessee	South Carolina	ICMA
Number of traffic related fatalities divided by police per 1,000 service area population			•	
Number of accident reports divided by police per 1,000 service area population			•	
Number of incident reports divided by police per 1,000 service area population			•	
Number of parking tickets divided by police per 1,000 service area population			•	
Police FTEs per 1,000 population		•		•
Sworn FTEs per 1,000 population				•
Civilian FTEs per 1,000 population				•
FTEs per road mile		•		
FTEs per square mile		•		
Number of neighborhoods active in crime watch programs			•	
Number of crime prevention and awareness structured programs			•	
Number of victims served in the victims/ witness advocacy program			•	
Efficiency Measures—Police Services				
Total number of cases assigned to investigative unit divided by number of officers assigned to criminal			•	
Part I cases cleared per sworn officer	•[1]			
UCR part I crimes (violent) cleared per sworn FTE				•
UCR part I crimes (property) cleared per sworn FTE				•
Incoming calls per FTEs		•		
Calls dispatched per sworn officer	•			
Calls for police patrol services divided by total patrol and traffic officers			•	
Dispatched calls per FTEs		•		
Response time from call to dispatch (citizen generated) in minutes			•	

Efficiency Measures— Police Services (continued)	North Carolina	Tennessee	South Carolina	ICMA
Average response time from dispatch to scene (citizen generated)			•	
Operating and maintenance expenditures charged to the police department per UCR part I crime cleared				•
Cost per dispatched police call	•	•		
Cost per part I case cleared	•			
Total cost for all police services divided by total police or public safety employees			•	
Total cost for all police services divided by service area total square miles			•	
Total cost for all police services divided by service area population			•	
Total operating and maintenance expenditures charged to the police department per capita				•
Police patrol cost per 1,000 population		•		
Cost per FTEs		•		
Sum of salary and benefits for both full-time and part-time employees			•	
Operating expenses divided by total police or public safety employees			•	
Depreciation (capitalized) expenses divided by total police or public safety employees			•	
Total direct and indirect costs to manage victims/witness advocacy program			•	
Total cost per victim served—victims/witness advocacy program			•	
Total cost for police and fire services including indirect and direct costs			•	
Total cost per certified full-time firefighter and full-time sworn officer (including public safety officers and volunteers)			•	
Effectiveness Measures—Police Services				
Traffic injury to accidents ratio		•		
Response time to high priority calls, minutes	•			

Effectiveness Measures— *Police Services (continued)*	*North* *Carolina*	*Tennessee*	*South* *Carolina*	*ICMA*
Response time in minutes to top priority calls (from receipt of call to dispatch)				•
Response time in minutes to top priority calls (from dispatch to arrival)				•
Total response time in minutes to top priority calls				•
Percent of part I cases cleared of those reported	•		•	•
Percent change in UCR part I reported crime from 2000 to 2001			•	
Percent change in criminal domestic violence arrests from 2000 to 2001			•	
Quality Measures—Police Services				
Citizens' response to survey question about direct contact with a city police officer			•	
Citizens' rating in survey of quality of law enforcement services			•	
Citizens' response to "how safe do you feel being alone in your neighborhood at night?"			•	
Citizens' perceptions of crime rate in neighborhood over last year			•	
Residents' rating of the quality of their contact with police during past 12 months				•
Citizens' rating of safety in their neighborhoods during the day				•
Citizens' ratings of safety in their neighborhoods after dark				•
Citizens' ratings of safety in business areas during the day				•
Citizens' ratings of safety in business areas after dark				•
Measures for Fire Services	*North* *Carolina*	*Tennessee*	*South* *Carolina*	*ICMA*
Inputs				
Actual fires per 1,000 population	•			

Inputs—Fire Services (continued)	*North Carolina*	*Tennessee*	*South Carolina*	*ICMA*
All direct costs plus indirect costs for fire services			•	
All direct costs plus indirect costs for fire services divided by fire per 1,000 service area population			•	
City appraised value (millions)		•		
City area square miles		•		
City road miles		•		
Daytime population				•
Emergency calls for service		•		
EMS calls		•		
EMS population density				•
EMS service level		•		
EMS square miles served				•
False alarms as percentage of total structure fire incidents and total fire incidents				•
Fire calls	•	•		
Fire department responses per 1,000 population	•			
Fire equipment and minimum staffing per apparatus				•
Fire incidents involving nonstructures per 1,000 population served				•
Form of government				•
ISO rating	•	•	•	
ISO rating outside city (if applicable)			•	
Land area served	•			
Land use of square miles served (percent agricultural/open space)				•
Land use of square miles served (percent commercial/industrial)				•
Land use of square miles served (residential)				•
Median household income				•
Nonemergency calls for service		•		

Inputs—Fire Services (continued)	North Carolina	Tennessee	South Carolina	ICMA
Number of engine companies	•			
Number of fire stations	•			•
Number of FTEs	•	•		
Paid fire and EMS staffing per 1,000 population served				•
Patients with full cardiac arrest from medical causes and patients who received early defibrillation				•
Percentage below poverty level				•
Percentage juveniles in service area				•
Percentage of patients in full cardiac arrest who have specified rhythms upon delivery to a medical facility				•
Percentage owner-occupied housing in city				•
Percentage unemployed in city				
Population density fire suppression services				•
Population inside city			•	
Population outside city			•	
Population served	•			•
Residential arson incidents per 10,000 residents served				•
Residential population				•
Residential population served EMS services				•
Residential structure fires per 1,000 population served				•
Salaries and benefits for full- and part-time fire employees divided by fires per 1,000 service area population			•	
Service area inside city—square miles			•	
Service area outside city—square miles			•	
Services provided to areas beyond jurisdiction boundary				•
Services provided to areas smaller than jurisdiction boundary				•

Inputs—Fire Services (continued)	*North Carolina*	*Tennessee*	*South Carolina*	*ICMA*
Square miles				•
Structure fires (number)	•	•		
Total arson incidents				•
Total arson incidents per 10,000 population				•
Total combined commercial and industrial structure fire incidents per 1,000 commercial and industrial structures				•
Total costs		•	•	
Total fire incidents per 1,000 population served				•
Total general fund operating expenses (millions)				•
Total number responses to residential structural fires divided by fires per 1,000 service area population			• [2]	
Total direct and indirect costs for police services plus total direct costs and indirect costs for fire services (total cost for police and fire services)			• [3]	
Total nonfire incidents per 1,000 population				•
Total residential structure fire incidents				•
Total residential structure fire incidents per 1,000 residential structures				•
Total service area population			•	
Total service area square miles			•	•
Total number of responses in each category divided by fires per 1,000 service area population			•	
Number of vehicle fires divided by fires per 1,000 service area population			•	
Number of single family structure fires divided by fires per 1,000 service area population			•	
Outputs/Workload—Fire Services				
Inspections by fire companies		•		
Fire code inspections by trained workers			•	

Outputs/Workload— Fire Services (continued)	North Carolina	Tennessee	South Carolina	ICMA
Fire code violations		•		
Fire loss ($)		•		
Number of multifamily fires divided by fires per 1,000 service area population			•	
Commercial structural fires divided by fires per 1,000 service area population			•	
Number of hazardous material incidences divided by fires per 1,000 service area population			•	
Hazmat incidents per 10,000 population				•
Number of other fires divided by fires per 1,000 service area population			•	
Total number of false alarms in each category divided by fires per 1,000 service area population			•	
Total number of medical responses in each category divided by fires per 1,000 service area population			•	
Rescues and recoveries performed per 10,000 population served				•
EMS responses per 1,000 population served: total, basic life support, and advanced life support responses				•
Fire personnel injuries with time lost				•
Fire personnel injuries with time lost per 1,000 incidents				•
Fire personnel injuries with time lost, FY 1999–2002				•
Fire safety and awareness classes conducted divided by fires per 1,000 service area population			•	
Education program attendees divided by fires per 1,000 service area population			•	
Efficiency Measures—Fire Services				
Inspections completed per inspector FTE	•			
Fire inspections per 1,000 population	• [4]	•		
Arson clearance rate				•

Efficiency Measures— Fire Services (continued)	North Carolina	Tennessee	South Carolina	ICMA
Calls for service per 1,000 population		•		
Structure fires per 1,000 population		•		
Average response time, first unit on scene		•	•	
Average fire response time (exact minutes and seconds)			•	
Total fire operating and vehicle expenditures per capita				•
Fire services cost per 1,000 population		•		
Cost per response, all calls	•	•	•	
Total cost for fire services divided by per $1,000 appraised property value			•	
Total cost per certified full-time firefighter and full-time sworn officer			•	
Cost for fire services per certified full-time firefighter			•	
Operating expenditures divided by certified firefighters—including public safety officers			•	
Total cost for fire services divided by total service area square miles			•	
Total cost for fire services divided by total service area population			•	
Effectiveness Measures—Fire Services				
Percent of fire code violations cleared in 90 days	•			
Average medical response time in minutes and seconds			•	
Number of fire code violations corrected divided by total number of fire code violations discovered			•	
Percent fires for which cause is determined	•	•		
One- and two-family residential-structure fire incidents: fire out on arrival, confined to room of origin, or confined to structure of origin				•
Percent fires confined to room(s) involved on arrival	•			

Effectiveness Measures— *Fire Services (continued)*	*North* *Carolina*	*Tennessee*	*South* *Carolina*	*ICMA*
Average response time to priority one calls (minutes)	•			
Average medical response time from call to dispatched unit arrival			•	
EMS response time: average time from dispatch to arrival on scene for calls requiring lights and sirens response				•
Percentage of total fire calls with a response time of 5 minutes and under from dispatch to arrival on the scene				•
Percentage of total fire calls with a response time of 5 minutes and under from dispatch to arrival on the scene, FY 1999–2002				•
Percentage of total fire calls with a response time of 8 minutes and under from call entry to arrival on scene				•
Fire code violations, percent cleared		•		
Quality Measures—Fire Services				
Citizens' rating in opinion survey of quality of fire services			•	
Citizens' familiarity with city emergency medical services			•	
Citizens' rating of quality of emergency medical services provided by city			•	
Customer satisfaction among those having contact with fire and EMS within the past 12 months				•
Citizens' response to "have you heard or read any city fire department material related to fire prevention?"			•	
Measures for Solid Waste Services	*North* *Carolina*	*Tennessee*	*South* *Carolina*	*ICMA*
Inputs				
City area (square miles)		•		
City road miles		•		
Collection frequency	•	•	•	
Collection location(s)	•	•		

Inputs—Solid Waste Services (continued)	North Carolina	Tennessee	South Carolina	ICMA
Crew size (most commonly used)	•			
Daytime population				•
Direct cost for residential garbage collection plus indirect cost for residential garbage collection			•	
Direct cost plus indirect cost for commercial solid waste collection			•	
Direct cost plus indirect cost for residential trash, yard waste, and leaf collection			•	
Distance to landfill	•			
Service profile data	•			
Form of government				•
Median household income				•
Number of FTEs	•	•	•	
Number of roll-carts			•	
Number of trips per day to landfill	•			
Percent of service contracted	•			
Percentage below poverty level				•
Percentage owner-occupied housing in city				•
Percentage unemployed				•
Population size of city		•		•
Population density				•
Refuse collection service features				•
Refuse disposal features				•
Residential collection points	•	•	•	
Residential refuse collected (tons)	•	•		
Service area population			•	
Service area in total square miles			•	
Square miles of city				•
Total costs		•	•	
Total general fund operating expense (millions)				•
Outputs/Workload—Solid Waste Services				
Tons of refuse collected per 1,000 population	•	•[5]		

Outputs/Workload— Solid Waste Services (continued)	North Carolina	Tennessee	South Carolina	ICMA
Tons of refuse collected per 1,000 collection points	•	•[6]	•	
Requests per 1,000 collection points		•[7]		
Average tons of refuse collected per refuse collection account—all account types				•
Number of commercial solid waste tons collected			•	
Number of residential trash tons collected plus number of residential yard waste and leaf tons collected divided by per 1,000 collection points			•	
Efficiency Measures—Solid Waste Services				
Average cost per collection point: backdoor		•		
Average cost per collection point: curbside		•		
Cost per residential collection point	•	•	•	
Cost per ton collected at backdoor		•		
Cost per ton collected curb side		•		
Cost per ton of refuse collected	•	•	•	
Operating and maintenance expenditures for refuse collection and disposal per account—all account types				•
Operating and maintenance expenditures for refuse collection per refuse collection account				•
Operating and maintenance expenditures for refuse collection per ton of refuse collected				•
Collection points multiplied by collection frequency divided by number of FTEs assigned to residential waste collection multiplied by average number hours worked per week			•	
Cost per collection point for residential trash, yard wastes, and leaf collection			•	
Cost per ton of commercial solid wastes collected (dumpsters only)			•	
Cost per ton residential trash, yard wastes, and leaves collected			•	

Efficiency Measures— Solid Waste Services (continued)	North Carolina	Tennessee	South Carolina	ICMA
Direct cost plus indirect cost for commercial solid waste collection			•	
Number of tons of garbage from residences and small businesses using roll-carts divided by number of FTEs			•	
Number of tons of residential trash, yard wastes, and leaves collected per assigned FTE			•	
Tons collected per FTE	•	•		
Total cost for all solid waste services			•	
Total cost per collection of all solid waste services			•	
Effectiveness Measures—Solid Waste Services				
Complaints per 1,000 collection points	•			
Requests per 1,000 collection points		•		
Valid complaints per 1,000 collection points	•			
Quality Measures—Solid Waste Services				
Citizens' rating in opinion survey of quality of garbage collection services			•	•
Citizens' response in opinion survey to question about familiarity with yard waste collection services			•	
Citizens' rating in opinion survey of quality of residential trash, waste, and leaf collection services provided by the city			•	

Measures for Household Recycling	North Carolina	Tennessee	South Carolina	ICMA
Inputs				
Collection frequency	•		•	
Collection points	•			
Daytime population				•
Direct cost for residential recycling collection plus indirect cost for residential recycling (excludes tipping fees)			•	
Direct cost plus indirect cost for recycling disposal of processing (includes tipping fees)			•	

Inputs—Household Recycling (continued)	North Carolina	Tennessee	South Carolina	ICMA
Drop-off centers (city owned)	•		•	
Form of government				•
FTE collection positions	•		•	
Facilities features				•
Median household income				•
Percent service contracted	•			
Percent population below poverty level				•
Percentage of juveniles in city				•
Percentage owner-occupied housing				•
Percent unemployed				•
Population density				•
Recyclables sorted at curb policy	•		•	
Residential population				•
Square miles				•
Tons collected	•			
Total general fund operating expenses (in millions)				•
Outputs/Workload—Household Recycling				
Average tons of recyclable material collected per account				•
Number of tons of residential recyclables collected per 1,000 collection points			•	
Tons of recyclables per 1,000 population	•			
Tons of solid waste land filled per 1,000 population	•			
Efficiency Measures—Household Recycling				
Cost per collection point	•		•	
Cost per ton collected	•		•	
Number of tons of residential recyclables collected divided by the number of FTEs and inmates			•	
Operating and maintenance expenditures for recycling services per ton of recyclable material collected				•

Efficiency Measures— Household Recycling (continued)	North Carolina	Tennessee	South Carolina	ICMA
Operating and maintenance expenditures for recycling services per account				•
Tons collected per FTE	•			
Total cost per ton of recyclables processed or disposed (includes tipping fees)			•	
Effectiveness Measures—Household Recycling				
Number of tons of residential recyclables collected divided by total tons garbage and recyclables collected			•	
Percent of waste stream diverted from landfill by recycling	•			
Set-out rate	•			
Tons of recyclable material collected as a percentage of all refuse and recyclable material collected				•
Tons recycled as a percentage of tons of residential refuse plus tons recycled	•			
Quality Measures—Household Recycling				
Citizens' response in opinion survey to question about familiarity with city recycling services			•	
Citizens' rating of residential recycling services in opinion survey				•
Citizens' rating in opinion survey of the quality of recyclable collection services provided			•	

* The ICMA does not classify measures as either input, workload, efficiency, effectiveness, or quality; all ICMA measures were placed in categories by the author.
[1] North Carolina classifies Part I Case Cleared Per Sworn Officer as both an efficiency and an effectiveness measure; the author classifies it as an efficiency measure.
[2] South Carolina classifies total number of responses to residential structural fires divided by fires per 1,000 service area as an output; the author classifies it as an input.
[3] South Carolina classifies all direct costs plus indirect costs for police services plus all direct costs plus indirect costs for fire services (total cost for police and fire services) as an efficiency measure; the author classifies it as an input.
[4] North Carolina classifies fire inspections per 1,000 population as a workload measure; the author classifies it as an efficiency measure.
[5] Tennessee classifies tons of refuse collected per 1,000 population as efficiency measures; the author classifies it as an output.
[6] Tennessee classifies tons of refuse collected per 1,000 collection points as an efficiency measure; the author classifies it as an output or workload measure.
[7] Tennessee classifies service requests per 1,000 collection points as an effectiveness measure. The author has grouped this measure in the output/workload category.

Appendix B

FINANCIAL DATA COLLECTION FORMS FOR THE TENNESSEE MUNICIPAL BENCHMARKING PROJECT

FORM A: COST OF PERSONAL SERVICES

DEPARTMENT: CITY:

Code	Account	Account Definition	FY 2004 ($)
1	Salaries and wages— full-time Includes holiday pay	Gross earnings of full-time/ permanent employees subject to FICA and retirement regulations	
2	Salaries and wages— part-time	Gross earnings of part-time/ temporary employees subject to FICA but not retirement regulations	
3	Overtime pay	Overtime and holiday pay	
4	Other pay	All other pay	
5	FICA taxes	Department's share of FICA taxes on all wages	
6	Insurance and hospitalization	Department's share of hospitalization and medical insurance	
7	Retirement contributions	Department's share of retirement plan contributions	

			FY 2004
Code	*Account*	*Account Definition*	*($)*
8	Insurance—workmen's compensation	Department's share of workmen's compensation insurance paid to employees. If self-insured, the actual medical costs and compensation paid for lost time from job-related accidents	
9	Unemployment taxes	Department's share of state unemployment taxes	
10	Other employee benefits	Department's share of any other employee benefits	
11	Other employer contributions	Department's share of any other employer contributions	

DEPARTMENT: CITY:

PERSONAL SERVICES TOTAL:

FORMS B1 (Items 12–22) and B2 (Items 23–29): OPERATING EXPENSES

DEPARTMENT: CITY:

			FY 2004
Code	*Account*	*Account Definition*	*($)*
12	Printing/ publications/postage	Includes all direct costs of printing, publications, postage, delivery charges, and other transportation costs	
13	Advertising	Includes all direct costs of advertising	
14	Dues and subscriptions	Includes all direct costs of subscriptions, registration fees, dues, and memberships	
15	Telephone	Includes all direct and indirect costs for local and long distance telephone services, including pagers	
16	Utilities	Includes all direct costs for electric, water, sewer, gas, or other fuels used to provide utility service; includes any indirect costs	

			FY 2004
Code	*Account*	*Account Definition*	*($)*
17	Professional and contractual services	Includes all direct costs of legal, medical, engineering, accounting, auditing, or other professional services	
18	Data processing and GIS	Includes all direct costs of data processing, MIS, GIS, and similar services	
19	Fleet maintenance	All direct costs for fleet maintenance	
20	Equipment maintenance	Includes all direct costs for office machines, equipment, and maintenance contracts	
21	Buildings and grounds maintenance	All direct costs for building and property maintenance, includes janitorial services, repairs	
22	Training and travel expenses	Includes all direct training and travel costs except registration fees	
23	Fees and licenses	Includes all direct costs of fees, license, and permits, including jail fees	
24	Uniforms	Includes all direct costs for uniform purchases or gear purchased or rented for employees	
25	Supplies—operating	Includes direct costs of all supplies except supplies for resale; includes office and operating supplies and noncapital purchases	
26	Supplies—for resale	Includes all direct costs for purchases of supplies or items for resale	
27	Contract administration	Includes all direct costs the department incurs for contract administration	
28	Rents	Includes all direct costs for building and equipment rent; any equipment lease that is not capitalized goes here	

DEPARTMENT: CITY:

			FY 2004
Code	*Account*	*Account Definition*	*($)*
29	Other operating expenses	Includes all direct costs not captured in another category	

OPERATING EXPENSES TOTAL:

FORMS C1 *(Items 30–36)* C2 *(Items 37–43)*: INDIRECT COSTS

DEPARTMENT: *CITY:*

			FY 2004
Code	*Account*	*Account Definition*	*($)*
30	Insurance—building and property	Department's percentage of building and property insurance costs and/or direct costs of this insurance, based on square footage occupied	
31	Insurance—equipment and vehicles	Department's percentage of equipment and vehicle insurance costs and/or direct costs of this insurance; allocation based on number of vehicles	
32	Insurance—liability	Department's percentage of liability insurance costs and/or direct costs of this insurance; allocation usually based on the number of FTEs in the department divided by the number of FTEs in the city	
33	Insurance—workmen's compensation	Department's percentage of workmen's compensation insurance costs and/or direct costs of this insurance; usually based on FTEs	
34	Insurance—other	Includes any insurance costs not captured elsewhere	
35	Central data processing	Allocation based on the department's percentage of computers; do not duplicate costs recorded on line 18	
36	Personnel/payroll	Define resources costs devoted to payroll; allocation based on the department's number of FTEs	

			FY 2004
Code	Account	Account Definition	($)
37	Personnel/benefits	Define resource costs devoted to benefits administration; allocation based on department's number of FTEs	
38	Accounts payable	Define resource costs devoted to accounts payable; allocation based on department's number of nonpayroll checks	
39	Purchasing	Define resource costs devoted to purchasing; allocation based on department's number of purchase orders	
40	Shared building costs	Define building costs for shred facilities; allocation based on department's square footage occupied	
41	Shared equipment maintenance costs	Define shared equipment maintenance (i.e., central garage); explain method of allocation	
42	Shared fleet maintenance	Define fleet maintenance expenses for the department	
43	Risk management	If the city has a risk management function, allocate department's share and explain allocation method	

DEPARTMENT: *CITY:*

INDIRECT EXPENSES TOTAL:

FORM D: DEPRECIATION—Use calculated depreciation in categories below based on GASB 34 capital asset records.

DEPARTMENT: *CITY:*

			FY 2004
Code	Account	Account Definition	($)
44	Depreciation	Buildings	
45	Depreciation	Improvements other than buildings	
46	Depreciation	Equipment	

Code	Account	Account Definition	FY 2004 ($)
DEPARTMENT:		CITY:	
47	Depreciation	Autos and light vehicles	
48	Depreciation	Medium and heavy equipment	
49	Depreciation	Other capital assets	
DEPRECIATION EXPENSES TOTAL:			

FORM E: SUMMARY OF EXPENSES

	FY 2004 ($)
DEPARTMENT: CITY:	
PERSONAL SERVICES EXPENSES TOTAL	
OPERATING EXPENSES TOTAL	
INDIRECT EXPENSES TOTAL	
DEPRECIATION EXPENSES TOTAL	
TOTAL EXPENSES:	

Bibliography

Aberbach, Joel D., and Bert A. Rockman. "Mandates or Mandarins? Control and Discretion in the Modern Administrative State." *Public Administration Review* 48, no. 2 (1988): 606–12.

Abney, Glenn, and Thomas P. Lauth. *The Politics of State and City Administration.* Albany: State University of New York Press, 1986.

Ammons, David N. *Municipal Benchmarks: Assessing Local Performance and Establishing Community Standards.* Thousand Oaks, Calif.: Sage Publications, 2001.

———. "Performance Measurement and Managerial Thinking." *Public Performance and Management Review* 25, no. 4 (2002): 344–47.

———. "A Proper Mentality for Benchmarking." *Public Administration Review* 59, no. 2 (1999): 105–9.

Ammons, David N., Charles Coe, and Michael Lombardo. "Performance Comparison Projects in Local Government: Participants' Perspectives." *Public Administration Review* 61, no. 1 (2001): 100–110.

Babakus, Emin, and Gregory W. Boller. "An Empirical Assessment of the SERVQUAL Scale." *Journal of Business Research* 24 (1992): 253–68.

Banfield, Edward C., and James Q. Wilson. *City Politics.* New York: Vintage Press, 1963.

Banovetz, James M., Drew A. Dolan, and John W. Swain. *Managing Small Cities and Counties: A Practical Guide.* Washington, D.C.: ICMA Press, 1994.

Behn, Robert D. "The Big Questions in Public Management." *Public Administration Review* 55, no. 4 (1995): 313–24.

Beierle, Thomas C., and Jerry Cayford. *Democracy in Practice: Public Participation in Environmental Decisions.* Washington, D.C.: Resources for the Future, 2002.

Booth, David A. *Council-Manager Government in Small Cities.* Washington, D.C.: ICMA Press, 1968.

Bosworth, Karl L. "The Manager Is a Politician." *Public Administration Review* 18, no. 3 (1958): 216–22.

157

Bowers, James R., and Wilbur C. Rich, eds. *Governing Middle-Sized Cities: Studies in Mayoral Leadership*. Boulder, Colo.: Rienner, 2000.

Brown, Stephen W., and Teresa A. Swartz. "A Gap Analysis of Professional Service Quality." *Journal of Marketing* 53 (April 1989): 92–98.

Bureau of Labor Statistics. www.bls.gov/news.release/pdf/union2.pdf (accessed 26, 2004).

Byrsland, Alexandra, and Adrienne Curry. "Service Improvements in Public Services Using SERVQUAL." *Managing Service Quality* 11, no. 6 (2001): 389–401.

Chakrapani, Chuck. *How to Measure Service Quality and Customer Satisfaction: An Informal Field Guide for Tools and Techniques*. Chicago: American Marketing Association, 1998.

Chambliss, Daniel F., and Russell Schutt. *Making Sense of the Social World: Methods of Investigation*. Thousands Oaks, Calif.: Sage, 2003.

Chase, Gordon, and Elizabeth C. Reveal. *How to Manage in the Public Sector*. Boston: McGraw-Hill, 1983.

Clarke, Susan E., and Gary Gaile. *The Work of Cities*. Minneapolis: University of Minnesota Press, 1998.

Coe, Charles K. "Local Government Benchmarking: Lessons from Two Major Efforts." *Public Administration Review* 59, no. 2 (1999): 100–115.

———. "A Report on Report Cards." *Public Performance and Management Review* 27, no. 2 (2003): 53–76.

Coe, Charles K., and Deborah Lamm Wiesel. "Police Budgeting: Winning Strategies." *Public Administration Review* 61, no. 6 (2001): 718–27.

Cohen, Steven, and William Eimicke. *Tools for Innovators: Creative Strategies for Managing Public Sector Organizations*. San Francisco: Jossey-Bass, 1998.

Commission on Accreditation for Law Enforcement Agencies, Inc. www.calea.org (accessed October 7, 2004).

———. www.calea.org/agcysearch/searchagcy1.cfm (accessed October 7, 2004).

Cronin, Joseph, Jr., and Steven Taylor. "SERVPERF Versus SERVQUAL: Reconciling Performance-Based and Perceptions Minus Expectations Measurement of Service Quality." *Journal of Marketing* 58 (January 1994): 125–31.

DeHoog, Ruth Hoogland, and Gordon P. Whitaker. "Political Conflict or Professional Advancement: Alternative Explanations for City Manager Turnover." *Journal of Urban Affairs*, 12, no. 4 (1990): 361–77.

Dunn, Delmer D., and Jerome Legge Jr. "Politics and Administration in U.S. Local Governments." *Journal of Public Administration Research and Theory* 12, no. 3 (2002): 401–22.

Dye, Thomas R., and John A. Garcia. "Structure, Function, and Policy in American Cities." *Urban Affairs Quarterly* 14, no. 1 (1978): 103–23.

Environmental Protection Agency. www.epa.gov/epaoswer/nonhw/muncpl/recycle .htm#Figures (accessed October 12, 2004).

Farnham, Paul G. "The Impact of Government Functional Responsibility on Local Expenditure." *Urban Affairs Quarterly* 22, no. 1 (1986): 151–65.

Federal Bureau of Investigation. "Crime in the United States." In *Uniform Crime Reports*. Washington, D.C.: U.S. Government Printing Office, 1999.

Federal Register of the United States Government. 65, no. 249 (December 27, 2000).

Feiock, Richard C., and James Clingermayer. "Municipal Representation, Executive Power, and Economic Development Policy Activity." *Policy Studies Journal* 15 (1986): 211–29.

Feiock, Richard C., and Christopher Stream. "Explaining the Tenure of Local Government Managers." *Journal of Public Administration Research and Theory* 8, no. 1 (1998): 117–31.

Ferman, Barbara. *Governing the Ungovernable City: Political Skill, Leadership and the Modern Mayor.* Philadelphia: Temple University Press, 1985.

Folz, David H. "Service Quality and Benchmarking the Performance of Municipal Services." *Public Administration Review* 64, no. 2 (2004): 209–20.

———. *Survey Research for Public Administration.* Thousand Oaks, Calif.: Sage, 1996.

Font, Javier. "Quality Measurement in Spanish Municipalities." *Public Productivity and Management Review* 21, no. 1 (1997): 44–55.

Fredrickson, H. George, ed. *Ideal and Practice in Council-Manager Government.* 2nd ed. Washington, D.C.: ICMA Press, 1995.

———. *The Spirit of Public Administration.* San Francisco: Jossey-Bass, 1996.

Fredrickson, H. George, Gary Johnson, and Curtis Wood. *The Adapted City: Institutional Dynamics and Structural Change.* Armonk, N.Y.: M. E. Sharpe, 2004.

Fredrickson, H. George, Brett Logan, and Curtis Wood. "Municipal Reform in Mayor Council Cities: A Well Kept Secret." *State and Local Government Review* 35, no. 1 (2003): 7–14.

French, P. Edward, and David H. Folz. "Executive Behavior and Decision Making in Small U.S. Cities." *American Review of Public Administration* 34, no. 1 (2004): 52–66.

Golembiewski, Robert T., and Gerald T. Gabris. "Today's City Managers: A Legacy of Success-Becoming-Failure." *Public Administration Review* 54, no. 6 (1994): 525–30.

Goodsell, Charles T. *The Case for Bureaucracy: A Public Administration Polemic.* Washington, D.C: CQ Press, 2003.

Governmental Accounting and Standards Board. www.seagov.org/sea_gasb_project/com_stmt_two.shtml (accessed October 22, 2004).

Grimes, Michael D., Charles Bonjean, Larry Lyon, and Robert L. Lineberry. "Community Structure and Leadership Arrangements: A Multidimensional Analysis." *American Sociological Review* 41, no. 4 (1976): 706–25.

Halachmi, Arie, ed. *Performance and Quality Measurement in Government: Issues and Experiences.* Burke, Va.: Chatelaine Press, 1999.

Hansell, William H., Jr. "Council-Manager Government: Alive and Leading Today's Best-Managed Communities." *National Civic Review* 90, no. 1 (2001): 41–43.

———. *Evolution and Change Characterize Council-Manager Government.* Washington, D.C.: ICMA Press, 2004.

———. "Is It Time To 'Reform' the Reform?" *Public Management* 80, no. 12 (1998): 15–16.

———. "Professionalism in Local Government Administration." In *The Future of Local Government Administration,* edited by H. George Frederickson and John Nalbandian. Washington, D.C.: ICMA Press, 2002.

Hansen, Susan B. "Participation, Political Structure, and Concurrence." *American Political Science Review* 69, no. 4 (1975): 1181–99.

Hassett, Wendy L., and Douglas J. Watson. "Citizen Surveys: A Component of the Budgetary Process." *Journal of Public Budgeting, Accounting and Financial Management* 15, no. 4 (2003): 525–42.

Hatry, Harry P. *Performance Measurement.* Washington, D.C.: The Urban Institute Press, 1999.

Hatry, Harry P., Louis H. Blair, Donald M. Fisk, John M. Greiner, John R. Hall, and Phillip S. Schaeman. *How Effective Are Your Community Services?* Washington, D.C.: American Enterprise Institute, 1992.

Hays, Samuel P. "The Politics of Reform in Municipal Government in the Progressive Era." *Pacific Northwest Quarterly* 55 (October 1964): 157–89.

Ho, Alfred. "Perceptions of Performance Measurement and the Practice of Performance Reporting by Small Cities." *State and Local Government Review* 35, no. 2 (2003): 161–73.

Hobbs, Daniel. "How to Benchmark with Easily Available Resources: Ensure That You're Comparing Apples to Apples." *Public Management* 86, no. 8 (2004): 14–18.

Institute for Public Service and Policy Research. *South Carolina Municipal Benchmarking Project FY 2001 Annual Report.* Columbia: University of South Carolina, 2002.

Insurance Services Office. *ISO's PPC Program.* Jersey City, N.J.: ISO Properties, 2001.

———. www.iso.com (accessed October 13, 2004).

———. www.iso.com/studies_analyses/ppc_program/docs/p3.html (accessed October 13, 2004).

———. www.iso.com/studies_analyses/ppc_program/docs/p2.html (accessed October 13, 2004).

———. www.isomitigation.com/bcegs5.html#q1 (accessed October 13, 2004).

International City/County Management Association. *Code of Ethics,* at www2.icma.org/main/bc.asp?bcid=40&hsid=1&ssid1=17&ssid2=24 (accessed October 22, 2004).

———. www2.icma.org (accessed October 22, 2004).

———. *The Municipal Yearbook.* Washington, D.C.: ICMA, 1999.

———. *The Municipal Yearbook.* Washington, D.C.: ICMA, 2000.

———. *The Municipal Yearbook.* Washington, D.C.: ICMA, 2003.

———. *Performance Management: When Results Matter,* at www2.icma.org (accessed September 2, 2004).

International City/County Management Association Center for Performance Measurement. *Comparative Performance Measurement Data Report FY 2002.* International City/County Management Association, at www2.icma.org/ (accessed October 22, 2004).

———. *Comparative Performance Measurement FY 2002 Data Report.* Washington, D.C.: ICMA Press, 2003.

Judd, Dennis R. *The Politics of American Cities: Private Power and Public Policy.* Glenview, Ill.: Scott Foresman, 1988.

Julnes, Patria de Lancer, and Marc Holzer. "Promoting the Utilization of Performance Measures in Public Organizations: An Empirical Study of Factors Affecting Adoption and Implementation." *Public Administration Review* 61, no. 6 (2001): 693–708.

Kaplan, Robert S., and David P. Norton. "The Balanced Scorecard: Measures That Drive Performance." *Harvard Business Review* January–February (1992): 71–79.

Karnig, Albert K. "Private-Regarding Policy, Civil Rights Groups, and the Mediating Impact of Municipal Reforms." *American Journal of Political Science* 19, no. 1 (1975): 91–106.

Kearney, Richard C., and Carmine Scavo. "Reinventing Government in Reformed Municipalities: Manager, Mayor and Council Actions." *Urban Affairs Review* 37, no. 1 (2001): 43–66.

Keehley, Patricia, Steven Medlin, Laura Longmire, and Sue A. MacBride. *Benchmarking for Best Practices in the Public Sector: Achieving Performance Breakthroughs in Federal, State, and Local Agencies.* San Francisco: Jossey-Bass, 1997.

Keller, Lawrence, and Michael W. Spicer. "Political Science and Public Administration: A Necessary Cleft?" *Public Administration Review* 57, no. 3 (1997): 270–71.

Kelly, Janet M., and William C. Rivenbark. *Performance Budgeting for State and Local Government.* Armonk, N.Y.: M. E. Sharpe, 2003.

Kopczynski, Mary, and Michael Lombardo. "Comparative Performance Measurement: Insights and Lessons Learned from a Consortium Effort." *Public Administration Review* 59, no. 2 (1999): 124–34.

Lasswell, Harold D. *Politics: Who Gets What, When, and How?* New York: McGraw-Hill, 1936.

Lee, Haksik, Yongki Lee, and Dongkeun Yoo. "The Determinants of Perceived Service Quality and Its Relationship with Satisfaction." *Journal of Services Marketing* 14, no. 3 (2000): 217–31.

Liebert, Roland J. *Disintegration and Political Action: The Changing Functions of City Government in America.* New York: Academic Press, 1976.

———. "Municipal Functions, Structure, and Expenditures: A Re-analysis of Recent Research." *Social Science Quarterly* 54, no. 1 (1974): 765–83.

Lineberry, Robert L., and Edmund P. Fowler. "Reformism and Public Policies in American Cities." *American Political Science Review* 61, no. 3 (1967): 701–16.

Lineberry, Robert L., and Ira Sharkansky. *Urban Politics and Public Policy.* New York: Harper and Row, 1978.

Lowi, Theodore J. "Legitimizing Public Administration." *Public Administration Review* 53, no. 3 (1993): 261–64.

———. "Lowi Responds." *Public Administration Review* 55, no. 5 (1995): 490–94.

Lyons, William. "Reform and Response in American Cities: Structure and Policy Reconsidered." *Social Science Quarterly* 59, no. 2 (1978): 118–32.

Marks, Thomas C., Jr., and John F. Cooper. *State Constitutional Law.* St. Paul, Minn.: West Publishing, 1988.

Montjoy, Robert S., and Douglas J. Watson. "A Case for Reinterpreted Dichotomy of Politics and Administration as a Professional Standard in Council-Manager Government." *Public Administration Review* 55, no. 3 (1995): 231–39.

Morgan, David R., and Robert E. England. *Managing Urban America*. New York: Chatham House, 1999.

Morgan, David R., and John Pellissero. "Urban Policy: Does Structure Matter?" *American Political Science Review* 74, no. 4 (1980): 999–1006.

Mouritzen, Paul E., and James H. Svara. *Leadership at the Apex: Politicians and Administrators in Western Local Governments*. Pittsburgh, Pa.: University of Pittsburgh Press, 2002.

National Civic League. www.ncl.org (accessed October 22, 2004).

Newell, Charldean, and David N. Ammons. "Role Emphases of City Managers and Other Municipal Executives." In *Ideal and Practice in Council-Manager Government*, edited by H. George Fredrickson, 97–107. Washington, D.C.: ICMA Press, 1995.

Newland, Chester A. "Managing from the Future in Council-Manager Government." In *Ideal and Practice In Council-Manager Government*, edited by H. George Fredrickson, 263–83. Washington, D.C.: ICMA Press, 1995.

North Carolina Local Government Performance Measurement Project. *Final Report on City Services for Fiscal Year 2002–2003*. Chapel Hill: University of North Carolina Institute of Government, February 2004.

Northrup, Alana, and William H. Dutton. "Municipal Reform and Group Influence." *American Journal of Political Science* 22, no. 3 (1978): 691–711.

Northwest Municipal Conference. *Bright Ideas: A Project of the NWMC Best Practices Committee*. Chicago: Northwest Municipal Conference, 2004.

Oliver, Richard L. "A Cognitive Model of the Antecedents and Consequences of Satisfaction Decisions." *Journal of Marketing Research* 17 (November 1980): 460–69.

O'Toole, Lawrence J. "Doctrines and Developments: Separation of Powers, the Politics-Administration Dichotomy, and the Rise of the Administrative State." *Public Administration Review* 47, no. 1 (1987): 17–25.

Parasuraman, A., Valarie A. Zeithaml, and Leonard L. Berry. "Alternative Scales for Measuring Service Quality: A Comparative Assessment Based on Psychometric and Diagnostic Criteria." *Journal of Retailing* 70, no. 3 (1994): 210–30.

———. "Reassessment of Expectations as a Comparison Standard in Measuring Service Quality: Implications for Further Research." *Journal of Marketing* 58 (January 1994): 111–24.

Parks, Roger B. "Linking Objective and Subjective Measures of Performance." *Public Administration Review* 44, no. 2 (1984): 118–27.

Parrado-Diez, Salvador, and Joaquin Ruiz-Lopez. "The Path of Quality in a Spanish Autonomous Agency." *Public Productivity and Management Review* 21, no. 1 (1997): 56–69.

Poister, Theodore H., and Gregory Streib. "Performance Measurement in Municipal Government: Assessing the State of the Practice." *Public Administration Review* 59, no. 4 (1999): 325–35.

Renner, Tari, and Victor S. DeSantis. "Municipal Form of Government: Issues and Trends." In *The Municipal Yearbook,* 30–41. Washington, D.C.: ICMA Press, 1998.

Rich, Michael J., Michael W. Giles, and Emily Stern. "Collaborating to Reduce Poverty: Views From City Halls and Community-Based Organizations." *Urban Affairs Review* 37, no. 2 (2001): 184–204.

Riordon, William L. *Plunkitt of Tammany Hall: A Series of Very Plain Talks on Very Practical Politics.* Boston: St. Martin's, 1994.

Rivenbark, William C., and Janet M. Kelly. "Management Innovation in Smaller Municipal Government." *State and Local Government Review* 35, no. 3 (2003): 196–205.

Ruchelman, Leonard I. *Big City Mayors: The Crisis in Urban Politics.* Bloomington: Indiana University Press, 1969.

Rust, Roland T., and Richard L. Oliver, eds. *Service Quality: New Directions in Theory and Practice.* Thousand Oaks, Calif.: Sage, 1994.

Scheuing, Eberhand E., and William F. Christopher, eds. *The Service Quality Handbook.* New York: American Management Association, 1993.

Schumaker, Paul, and Russell W. Getter. "Structural Sources of Unequal Responsiveness to Group Demands in American Cities." *The Western Political Quarterly* 36, no. 1 (1983): 7–29.

South Carolina Municipal Benchmarking Project. *2001 Fire Report,* Columbia: The University of South Carolina Institute for Public Service and Policy Research, 2002.
———. *2001 Police Report.* Columbia: The University of South Carolina Institute for Public Service and Policy Research, 2002.
———. *2001 Solid Waste Report.* Columbia: The University of South Carolina Institute for Public Service and Policy Research, 2002.

Sperling, Bert. *Sperling's Best Places,* n.d., at bestplaces.net/city/compare.aspx (accessed July 9, 2004).

Stivers, Camilla. "The Listening Bureaucrat: Responsiveness in Public Administration." *Public Administration Review* 54, no. 4 (1994): 364–69.

Stone, Deborah A. *Policy Paradox and Political Reason.* Glenview, Ill.: Scott Foresman, 1988.

Stumm, Theodore J., and Matthew Corrigan. "City Managers: Do They Promote Efficiency?" *Journal of Urban Affairs* 20, no. 3 (1998): 343–51.

Stumpf, Bryan D. "Small Towns Facing Rapid Growth." *Proceedings, National Planning Conference,* 1999, at www.asu.edu/caed/proceedings99 (accessed July 19, 2004).

Sumek, Lyle J. "Turbulent Times Require Courageous Leaders." Presentation, Annual Conference of the Tennessee City Manager's Association, Gatlinburg, Tenn., October 24, 2002.

Svara, James H. "Complementarity of Politics and Administration as a Legitimate Alternative to the Dichotomy Model." *Administration and Society* 30, no. 6 (1999): 676–705.
———. "Dichotomy and Duality: Reconceptualizing the Relationship Between Policy and Administration in Council-Manager Cities." *Public Administration Review* 45, no. 1 (1985): 221–32.

———. "Do We Still Need Model Charters? The Meaning and Relevance of Reforms in the 21st Century." *National Civic Review* 90, no. 1 (2001): 19–33.

———. "The Myth of the Dichotomy: Complementarity of Politics and Administration in the Past and Future of Public Administration." *Public Administration Review* 61, no. 2 (2001): 176–83.

———. *Official Leadership in the City: Patterns of Conflict and Cooperation.* Oxford: Oxford University Press, 1990.

———. "The Politics-Administration Dichotomy Model as Aberration." *Public Administration Review* 58, no. 1 (1998): 51–58.

———. "The Shifting Boundary Between Elected Officials and City Managers in Large Council-Manager Cities." *Public Administration Review* 59, no. 1 (1999): 44–53.

———. "U.S. City Managers and Administrators in a Global Perspective." In *The Municipal Yearbook.* Washington, D.C.: ICMA Press, 1999.

Tennessee Municipal Benchmarking Project. *FY 2002 Annual Report.* Knoxville: The University of Tennessee Municipal Technical Advisory Service, 2003.

———. *FY 2003 Annual Report.* Knoxville: The University of Tennessee Municipal Technical Advisory Service, 2004.

Terry, Larry D. *Leadership of Public Bureaucracies: The Administrator as Conservator.* Thousand Oaks, Calif.: Sage, 1995.

Thomas, John C. *Public Participation in Public Decisions: New Skills and Strategies for Public Managers.* San Francisco: Jossey-Bass, 1995.

U.S. Census Bureau. "Summary File 1C." Table STF1, 2000, at factfinder.census.gov/servlet/ (accessed July 12, 2004).

U.S. Census Bureau. "Summary File 3." Table STF1, 2000, at factfinder.census.gov/servlet/ (accessed July 12, 2004).

Walters, Jonathan, Mark Abrahams, and James Fountain. "Managing for Results: An Overview." In *Reporting Performance Information: Suggested Criteria for Effective Communication,* 13–24. Washington, D.C.: Governmental Accounting and Standards Board, 2003. Available at www.seagov.org/aboutpmg/mfr_chap3.pdf (accessed October 22, 2004).

Watson, Douglas J., and Wendy L. Hassett. "Career Paths in America's Largest Council-Manager Cities." *Public Administration Review* 64, no. 2 (2004): 192–99.

Weaver, R. Kent, and Bert A. Rockman. *Do Institutions Matter? Government Capabilities in the United States and Abroad.* Washington, D.C.: Brookings Institution, 1993.

Welch, Susan, and Timothy Bledsoe. *Urban Reform and Consequences.* Chicago: University of Chicago, 1988.

Wholey, Joseph S. "Performance-Based Management: Responding to the Challenge." *Public Productivity and Management Review* 22, no. 3 (1999): 288–307.

Wholey, Joseph S., and Harry P. Hatry. "The Case for Performance Monitoring." *Public Administration Review* 52, no. 6 (1992): 604–10.

Wholey, Joseph S., and Kathryn Newcomer. *Improving Government Performance.* San Francisco: Jossey-Bass, 1989.

Williams, Frank P., Marilyn D. McShane, and Dale Sechrest. "Barriers to Effective Performance Review." *Public Administration Review* 54, no. 6 (1994): 537–42.

Winchester, Benjamin. *Media Messages of Rural: Lessons from Minnesota*. Morris: University of Minnesota Center for Small Towns, 2004.

Wisniewski, Mik. "Assessing Customer Satisfaction with Local Authority Services Using SERVQUAL." *Total Quality Management* 12, nos. 7–8 (2002): 995–1002.

———. "Managing Service Quality." *Total Quality Management* 11, no. 6 (2001): 380–88.

Wisniewski, Mik, and Mike Donnelly. "Measuring Service Quality in the Public Sector: The Potential for SERVQUAL." *Total Quality Management* 7, no. 4 (1996): 357–65.

Wright, Deil S. "The City Manager as a Development Administrator." In *Comparative Urban Research*, edited by Robert T. Daland, 203–48. Beverly Hills, Calif.: Sage, 1969.

Wu, Liangfu, and Larry Bruce. "Introduction of Dynamic Government Performance Measurement." *Northwest Municipal Conference Report 2004*. Des Plaines, Ill.: Northwest Municipal Conference, May 2004.

Yates, Douglas. *The Ungovernable City*. Cambridge: MIT Press, 1977.

Index

Building Code Effectiveness Grading
Schedule (BCEGS), 71–73, 84n37
building code enforcement services,
71–73; service quality of, 71–73
bureaucracy, 128

capacity: design, 26; of facilities and
services, 61–62
career paths of chief executives, 23, 25,
126
caretaker role, 40
causal direction, 55
Cayford, Jerry, 49n19, 157
Chakrapani, Chuck, 82n10, 158
Chambliss, Daniel F., 85n43, 158
charter types, 15–23
Chase, Gordon, 9n5, 10n13, 158
chief administrative officers (CAO),
3–4, 21–22, 34; appointment of, 16
chief executives, 11–28; career paths,
23, 126; characteristics of, 23–26,
decision making patterns, 39–44;
education levels, 24; experience, 24;
gender, 24; partisanship, 24; powers,
21, 23; responsibilities, 16, 22; roles,
34–38; tenure, 24; time allocation,
36–38
Christopher, William F., 30n28, 82n8,
163
Chung, Yeonsoo, 9n8
citizen complaints, 61
citizen participation, 73, 85n51
citizen perceptions: environmental
influences on, 56; of service
performance, 55–56; of service
quality, 55–64
citizen satisfaction, 55, 104–5
citizen service needs and expectations,
53–64
citizen surveys, 57, 66, 118, 123n46
citizens' opinions, 53
city functions, 67, 75, 81n3, 100
city managers: characteristics of, 23–26;
decision making patterns, 39–46;

impact on service quality levels,
75–80, 128–29; powers, 34–38;
responsibilities of, 39–41, 128–29;
role in performance measurement,
129–30
Clarke, Susan E., 30n28, 158
Clemson (S.C.), *103*
Cleveland (Tenn.), 108–10
Clingermayer, James, *41*, 49n16, 159
code of ethics, 25, 31n29, 160
Coe, Charles, 81n4, 84n34, 121n8,
121n10, 122n21, 122n32, 124n59,
124n61, 124n68, 157–58
Cohen, Steven, 81n2, 121n10, 121n19,
158
Collierville (Tenn.), 108–10
Commission on Accreditation for Law
Enforcement Agencies, Inc.
(CALEA), 66–67
communication gap, *56*, 62
comparative performance analysis, 64,
88; comparative statistics, 90–92,
117
comparing service performance, 87–112
conceptual model of service quality,
55–64
conflict, 9n9; in council-manager cities,
47; in mayor-council cities, 40, 47
consultation: between executives and
council, 42–43; between executives
and department heads, 42–43;
between executives and public,
42–43, 46; patterns of, 41–47, 128
continuous process improvement, 90–91
Cooper, John F., 29n9, 161
corporate style benchmarking, 91–92
Corrigan, Matthew, 81n3, 85n49, 163
cost accounting, 102, 114
council: characteristics of, 21–23;
powers of, 21–23; responsibilities of,
15–16
council-manager government, 15–23;
attributes of, *21*; cooperation in, 47;
employees per capita in, *21*, 22;

About the Authors

David H. Folz is a professor in the Department of Political Science at the University of Tennessee, Knoxville. He earned a bachelor of arts in history, a master of science in planning, and a Ph.D. in political science from the University of Tennessee. He teaches graduate seminars in public management and research methods in the University of Tennessee public administration program and undergraduate classes in state politics, political analysis, and public policy. His research interests include local government management, service performance, environmental policy and management, and survey research methods. He has published extensively in the *Public Administration Review*, the *American Review of Public Administration,* and the *State and Local Government Review* as well as in other journals. He is author of *Survey Research for Public Administration*. He is "Essays and Reviews" editor for the *State and Local Government Review* and serves on the national council for Pi Alpha Alpha, the public administration honor society. He has served in various administrative capacities with several small communities in the South and continues to be a frequent consultant to local, state, and federal agencies. He directed the University of Tennessee MPA program for over eleven years. He is a member of the International City/County Management Association and the American Society for Public Administration. He and his wife Brenda live in Farragut, Tennessee.

P. Edward French is a former town manager in Virginia and holds a Ph.D. in public policy and administration from Mississippi State University. He has taught in the public administration programs of the University of Tennessee, East Tennessee State University, and Appalachian State University. He has

175

published in the *American Review of Public Administration*, the *State and Local Government Review*, the *International Journal of Public Administration*, the *International Journal of Organization Theory and Behavior*, *Public Administration Quarterly*, and the *Journal of Public Budgeting, Accounting, and Financial Management*, among other journals. He is coauthor of *Understanding American Government*. Currently, he is a lecturer with the Department of Political Science at the University of Tennessee, Knoxville, where he teaches courses in public administration, public policy, and American government.